# The FINALITY of CHRIST

# The FINALITY

# of CHRIST

## Dow Kirkpatrick, editor

Prepared Under the Direction of the World Methodist Council

Published by Abingdon Press
**Nashville   New York**

THE FINALITY OF CHRIST

Copyright © 1966 by Abingdon Press

Library of Congress Catalog Card Number: 66-21190

SET UP, PRINTED, AND BOUND BY THE
PARTHENON PRESS, AT NASHVILLE,
TENNESSEE, UNITED STATES OF AMERICA

*to*
## CARL MICHALSON (1915-1965)

"free from the fear of death
because our life is lived toward God
and not toward our own erosive future"

# PREFACE

The Wesleyan Revival would not have been what it was without Aldersgate. Aldersgate, let us never forget, would not have been what it was without Oxford.

John Wesley wrote to his brother Charles late in his life (December 15, 1772): "I often cry out, *Vitae me redde priori!* [Give me back my former life.] Let me be again an Oxford Methodist! . . . I did then walk closely with God and redeem the time. But what have I been doing these thirty years? " [1]

What he had been doing those thirty years was riding the circuit! So Methodism at its best has always managed to combine circuit riding, Aldersgate, and Oxford.

On three occasions now (1958, 1962, 1965) Methodist theologians have come in from their "circuits" all over the world to return to Oxford. Lincoln College has served as the place of living study and fellowship for a hundred such persons at each of the Oxford Institutes on Methodist Theological Studies under the aegis of the World Methodist Council.

Mr. Wesley frequently referred to the founding purpose as stated in the statutes of his college, Lincoln, "ad propagandam Christianam fidem et extirpandas haereses." ("For propagating the Christian faith and extirpating heresies.") It can be stated with certainty that at the Third Oxford Institute no heresies were extirpated. Let us hope none were, however, propagated!

The theme for this study was deliberately chosen to tie in

[1] *The Letters of John Wesley, Standard Edition,* VI, 6.

with studies currently under way in the World Council of Churches. Thus the Institute not only brought together Methodists from all over the world, but brought world Methodism into vital relationship with world ecumenism. This is intended to be a clue to the manner in which confessionalism and ecumenicity can live together in fruitful tension.

A glance at the list of contributors to this volume will reveal the very high caliber of the entire project. We are grateful beyond ability to express for their faithfulness to the task. Dr. D. T. Niles, of Ceylon, set forth the issues involved in the theme. Miss Morna Hooker specified the biblical base of the claim. The Rev. David Jenkins added immeasurably to the breadth of the discussion by his presence and vivid insight.

What benefit would there be in a group of cloistered Methodists assuring one another regarding the finality of Christ? To put reality into the discussions certain non-Christians were present to challenge us by presenting views held by large portions of the earth's peoples. Our Buddhist monk, The Venerable Dr. H. Ratanasara, is from Ceylon; Mrs. Pamela M. Wylam, Sikh editor, is a British convert to Sikhism.

The Institute was fortunate in the presence of Professor A. J. Ayer, author of *Language, Truth and Logic* and other well-known works, who gave, with verve and brilliance, an informal address, not for publication, on the independence of ethics from theology. It was not possible in planning the Institute to arrange for an address by a Jewish scholar, but this omission has been supplied in this volume by a paper by Dr. Will Herberg on the question of how the Jew looks at Jesus. For this we are grateful.

On this kind of foundation and against this kind of challenge, then, three American theologians set themselves the task of reformulating the Christian claim for the finality of

Christ, each, of course, from his own particular perspective.

Dr. Gordon Rupp brings the whole to a conclusion by relating the claim to the continuing expression of Christ's person and work as set forth by the church in its ministry of Word and Sacrament. Amply documented by Wesley hymns, Reformation theology, and tied into the current discussions on union between British Methodism and the Church of England, the chapter has all the vitality of its author.

Principal A. Raymond George, with the able assistance of Sister Lillian Topping, served on the British side as joint secretary in the project and made real again Wesley's observation that the Methodist fellowship is no "rope of sand." Dr. Lee Tuttle, secretary at Lake Junaluska, North Carolina, of the World Methodist Council furnished generous and extensive assistance in the handling of a voluminous amount of correspondence necessary to such worldwide undertakings.

Abingdon Press has again made a contribution to the church through its willingness to put the Oxford Institute papers in print, as it did *The Doctrine of the Church*, which was the discussion of the 1962 theme. It is hoped that the use to which that volume and this one is put by Methodists and others in all parts of the world may justify this courage and patience.

As any member of the 1965 Institute takes this volume in hand he will remember first the presence and person of Carl Michalson, whose death in a November plane crash at Cincinnati, Ohio, left a dark vacancy in our hearts. As one who stood with Janet and Carl the night they married, I value the opportunity this volume gives to offer a gesture of affection for them. Carl's own words from p. 172 of this book, as reprinted on the dedication page, are a fitting memorial.

DOW KIRKPATRICK

Evanston, 1965

# CONTENTS

11

# 1

## THE CHRISTIAN CLAIM FOR THE
## FINALITY OF CHRIST

Many years ago, when my second son was quite a little
boy, I took him to the Dalada Maligawa, where the tooth of
the Buddha is kept as a relic. It is the most famous Buddhist
temple in Ceylon. In one corner of the temple is a huge statue
of the Buddha. When I explained to my son who the Buddha
was, he said to me, "Yes, and after he died, he would have
gone to Jesus Christ. What did Jesus Christ do to him?" When
Paul preached to the Athenians on Mars' Hill, his final declaration to them was, "[God] has fixed a day on which he will
judge the world in righteousness by a man whom he has ap-
pointed, and of this he has given assurance to all men by
raising him from the dead" (Acts 17:31). In the parable of
Jesus on the last judgment, it is the Son of man who comes in
his glory as the judge. (Matt. 25:31 ff.)

To speak of the finality of Jesus Christ is to speak specifically
of the man Jesus. It is to talk neither about the finality of the
Christ-experience, nor about the finality of the Christ-revelation,
but about Jesus Christ himself. The issue is not whether all
true religious experience is an experience of God in Jesus
Christ, nor whether Jesus Christ is the final and therefore
determinative revelation of God; but whether it is true that

God has set, in the world and among men, this man Jesus as final—him to whom they must hearken, him whom they must obey, him through whom they will live and by whom they will be judged. Is Paul right when he says, "For although . . . there are many 'gods' and many 'lords'—yet for us there is one God, the Father, from whom are all things and for whom we exist, and one Lord, Jesus Christ, through whom are all things and through whom we exist" (I Cor. 8:5-6)?

Some time ago, at an international student conference of theological students, I had a strange experience. I found myself listening to a discussion about Jesus Christ, only to find that the Jesus Christ they were talking about was simply a historical point of reference around whom a body of doctrine and ethics had been built. They kept on saying, this is the Jesus Christ whom through the centuries the church has believed in and proclaimed and whom Christians have experienced. But they denied that it was possible really to know what Jesus Christ was like or said or did, when he walked the earth in the flesh. There was a bare skeleton of events which could be attested to with certainty. The rest was claimed to be "proclamation." It is not my intention to go into this question at this time. But I do want to say that, if in any real measure it is not possible to get within hearing and seeing distance of the man Jesus, then talk about the finality of Jesus Christ is simply futile. The crux of the finality issue is whether or not in Jesus Christ men confront and are confronted by the transcendent God whose will they cannot manipulate, by whose judgment they are bound, and with whose intractable presence in their midst they must inevitably reckon.

As one lives and works with men of other faiths, one is made constantly aware not only of the fact that Christians have different beliefs from those who are not Christian, but also of the fact that they believe in a different way. The very act of faith is different. The basic reason for this is that the coordinates within which the graph of the Christian faith is plotted are quite different from the coordinates used in other religions and other systems of belief. It is not simply that the graphs themselves are different.

One basic difference is that whereas in all other religions the coordinates of faith are determined by the relation between the infinite and the finite, the eternal and the temporal, in Christianity they are determined by the relation between the universal and the particular. The scriptural testimony is not that Jesus Christ is a finite manifestation of the infinite, but that he is the universal become particular—the image of the invisible God (Col. 1:15). Jesus Christ is neither a darshana nor an avatar.

The point at issue is the difference between the different experiences of meeting God and the experience of the compulsive specific obedience which one has when one meets Jesus. Jesus of Nazareth, whenever he addressed men, addressed them with specific demands—leave your nets, take up your bed, sell what you have. He is still the same Jesus. The experience of meeting God which is known as the mystical experience, and which is testified to by the devotees in all religions, is best understood within the relation between the infinite and the finite. However, when one is talking about the finality of Jesus Christ, one is talking about how this mystical experience is pegged down to this earthly life. To paraphrase Paul, the particular consists "in the works he has prepared for us to walk in" (Eph. 2:10).

That which is being contended for is not the prestige of a particular place of meeting between God and man, but the peculiarity of what happens when men meet God in Jesus Christ. When Jesus announced that "the kingdom of God is at hand," and demanded of men that they "repent, and believe in the gospel" (Mark 1:14), he was asking not for some general response to the requirements of religion or morality, but for a specific commitment to a particular event and person. The religious man is one kind of man; a Christian disciple is another kind of man. There is no substitute for the "shattering" which takes place when men meet God at God's place and hour of appointment, and for the consequences in discipline and discipleship of that experience.

Attempts have certainly been made, again and again, to change this axis around which the Christian faith rotates, to change these coordinates within which the graph of that faith is plotted. There have always been those who have desired to understand the Christian faith, not in terms of the relation between the universal and the particular, but in terms of the relation between the infinite and the finite, the eternal and the temporal. In this discussion the crux of the argument has always been concerning the resurrection of Jesus Christ. The New Testament insistence on the decisive significance of the resurrection of Jesus Christ constitutes a denial of the view that Jesus is a temporal manifestation of the eternal God, a finite appearance of him who is infinite. The finite and the temporal are categories which apply to that which is repeatable. The resurrection faith, however, is concerned with the eternity and the universality of Jesus Christ himself. What the New Testament is announcing is not that the Christ-experience cannot be destroyed by death nor that the Christ-revelation includes a revelation of death as not final, but that Jesus himself rose from the dead. The testimony is not to the life of Jesus after death, but to his conquest of death. What the New Testa-

16

ment makes clear is that while the risen Christ offers himself only to the perception of faith, he is nevertheless to be proclaimed to all men as having risen from the dead. There is a happening apart from faith which is proclaimed, even though it is to faith that the proclamation is addressed. As Paul puts it, "[God] has given assurance to all men by raising him from the dead" (Acts 17:31). When Peter says, "This Jesus, . . . you crucified and killed. . . . But God raised him up" (Acts 2:23-24), he is talking not about something that had happened to the disciples, but about something that had happened to Jesus.

Also, even as by its testimony to the resurrection of Jesus Christ the New Testament witnesses to the eternity of the specific man Jesus, even so by its testimony to the ascension of Jesus Christ the New Testament seeks to say that in Jesus the distinction between the infinite and the finite is an irrelevant distinction. "Seated at the right hand of God" is a way of saying that here is the operative reality, the whole is present at this point and in this person, this is both the infinite and the finite, he is what God is with respect to all things—their Sovereign and Savior, their Judgment and their Judge.

Now we can see how it is that, while the New Testament testimony is to a specific event which happened, it is able also to speak of this event in the present tense. For precisely in the fact that the New Testament faith concerning Jesus Christ is stated unambiguously in terms of the relation between the universal and the particular lies the ground for the New Testament witness that Jesus Christ is the same yesterday, today, and for ever (Heb. 13:8). The finality that is asserted is not the finality of an event in the past or a person in the past, but the finality of him who is continuously and identifiably present. "He must reign until he has put all his enemies under his

17

feet." (I Cor. 15:25.) "I am with you always, to the close of the age." (Matt. 28:20.)

When God revealed himself to Moses, he revealed himself as one who was recognized by being continuously present, and by being known by that presence alone. (Exod. 3:14). Moses had to lead his people to follow a God who would never become past tense. The second commandment, "You shall not make yourself a graven image" (Exod. 20:4), is a commandment not to attempt to make God static. Indeed, no understanding of God which is delimited by a past tense is satisfactory. The attraction of thinking in terms of the infinite and the finite is that the finite can keep on repeating itself. There is no finality because there is constant progress and process. As the Bhagavad Gita has it, "Though unborn and immutable in essence, though Lord of Beings, yet governing Nature which is mine, I come into being by my delusive power. For whensoever right declines, O Bharata, and wrong uprises, then I create myself" (iv 6-7).

The biblical faith has a different thrust. The finality which is affirmed about Jesus Christ is set within the context of an ongoing activity of God, whereby the past does not remain past, but is continuously becoming present. In the Exodus passage to which reference has been made, it is the God of Abraham, Isaac, and Jacob who reveals himself to Moses as "I am." So also, the New Testament witness to the finality of Jesus Christ is not simply to the finality of a past event, but of a present Savior. It is the same bush which is burning without being consumed. When the church confesses, "And I believe in Jesus Christ—born, suffered, crucified, died, and buried; who rose again and has ascended and will come"—it is of the same Jesus that this confession is made. (Acts 1:11.) It is he who is final; not that everything is over, but that he encompasses everything that takes place. In the closing words of the Bible, as Jesus

18

speaks them, "I am the Alpha and the Omega, the first and the last, the beginning and the end" (Rev. 22:13).

This way of relating past tense to present tense takes the discussion from a consideration of the person of Christ to a consideration of his work. Mark gives to his gospel the title, "The beginning of the gospel of Jesus Christ." Luke says that in his gospel he recorded "all that Jesus began to do and teach" (Acts 1:1). When Jesus declared that the kingdom of God had come, there was a double thrust in that declaration. The event of the coming was past tense. But the kingdom of God itself was present continuous tense. The finality of Jesus Christ is the finality of an ongoing work.

This indissoluble connection between the person of Jesus Christ and his work, when speaking of his finality, leads to a clarification of a second basis of difference between the co-ordinates of the Christian faith and those of other faiths and beliefs. The scriptures of other religions deal fundamentally either with the interior life or the life after death. The Christian Scriptures, however, speak in the first instance about this present life in all its concreteness and its particularities. Other religions hold that the important thing in the drama of life is what happens to the actors, while the Christian Scriptures affirm that what happens to the actors is only a part of God's concern. His total concern encompasses the whole drama—men, women, and children, and all of nature, in their relationships to one another and in their several particularities of age and sex, of community and race, of nation and religion, and across the generations of time. It is this insistence on this world which gives to the New Testament declaration that in Jesus God became man its true context.

When the name of Jesus is announced as "Emmanuel"— "God with us" (Matt. 1:23), the announcement affirms the

19

"with-ness" of God on which human life depends. Man is
made in the image of God (Gen. 1:27). This imaging relationship, in which man is perpetually placed before God, constitutes
the meaning and responsibility of human life. The God-man
relationship is a treble one. "In him we live and move and
have our being." (Acts 17:28.) But this God, in whom we are,
is also the God who is within us. (Col. 1:27.) He is constantly
in our lives and within our personalities, seeking to evoke in us
a true response to himself. In the third place, that to which
response has to be made is also constantly present as the reality
of God outside us, impinging on us, both in wrath and in
mercy, both in judgment and in demand. (Rev. 3:20.) There
is no way of simplifying the God-man relationship, so that any
one of these three relations—God's inclusiveness, his imma-
nence, and his transcendence—is subsumed under the other
two. When Scripture testifies to the finality of Jesus Christ, it
is speaking of this fact of Jesus as Emmanuel, God with us, in
the richness of this threefold relation, and in so doing, bears
witness to the several aspects of the work of Christ.

1. The first strand in the biblical testimony to the work of
Jesus Christ is that it is *he from whom all things proceed and
receive their vocation.* Paul states this quite directly when he
says, "All things were created through him and for him" (Col.
1:16). Scripture does not find it a logical burden to attribute
to Jesus Christ the origin of things, because it sees clearly that
their meaning is in him. All things were not only made through
him, but nothing made is outside him. (John 1:3.) He is the
one in whom all things are, and who is in all things. Their true
nature and vocation is what he is in them and what they are in
him.

The significance of what is being said here lies in the fact
that, by this way of saying it, the Creator and his creation are
shown as being bound together. He through whom all things

20

were created is also the first born of all creation. (Col. 1:15-16.)
The whole of creation is invested with meaning because he is
part of them. In him the "with-ness" of God is affirmed. All
things are from him, and he is of them.

2. The natural next step in the biblical testimony is to speak
of Jesus Christ as *he in whom all things cohere and work together.* (Col. 1:17.) Everything keeps moving and changing,
and yet the whole thing holds together. Things do not fly
apart. Life remains a unity in spite of all its diversity. The
mystery of evil, too, is held within the exercise of God's sovereign grace. (II Thes. 2:7-8.) An inclusive purpose binds everything together, a purpose which belongs to someone in ultimate
authority. Men experience this ultimacy in personal life, as
they see how he rules and overrules all things, "in everything
[working] for good with those who love him" (Rom. 8:28);
while, in the life of society, this ultimacy is maintained and
declared through a mission. "All authority in heaven and on
earth," Jesus says, "has been given to me. Go therefore and
make disciples of all nations" (Matt. 28:18-19). The apostles
are sent everywhere and to everyone, because everywhere and
over everyone Jesus is already in authority. No wonder Paul
in his close-knit argument in his letter to the Romans, makes
Jesus Christ the key to the understanding of the whole of
history. No failure, he says, is final. No betrayal or disobedience
is ultimate. There is always a way out of what seems a blind
alley. No one is outside the overarching purposes of God. "O
the depth of the riches and wisdom and knowledge of God!
How unsearchable are his judgments and how inscrutable his
ways! . . . For from him and through him and to him are all
things." (Rom. 11:33-36.)

This way of stating the finality of Jesus rests on the fact that,
as he is part of creation and is himself involved in human
history, that which happened to him must become the source

21

of that which happens to all. He is "the pioneer of [our] salvation" (Hebrews 2:10). So that even as it is possible to speak of the whole as being infected by sin, we can speak of the whole as being infected by salvation. (I Cor. 15:21-22.) The pioneer does not set an example to be followed; he opens up a highway by which men can now go to the land that has been won for them by him.

3. However, the teaching of Scripture is not that in Jesus all is now well, and well anyhow. Jesus is *he by whom all things are judged and brought to judgment.* His finality bears a consequence for all things.

As John puts it, the fact that God has sent his son into the world sets before men a real choice—either to believe in him and so to share in eternal life—the life which he lives in the world—or to live apart from him and so to perish. (John 3:16.) That which has perished has no use. Just as a fruit which has perished is useless for eating, so he who has perished is of no use to Jesus Christ. And, conversely, to be of no use to Jesus Christ is to perish.

The point is that there is a determining reality in the world which is Jesus Christ at work in it. "In him was life, and the life was the light of men." (John 1:4.) This light has now come into the world. (John 1:9.) So that, the life he lives in the world becomes the way by which all men must walk, as it also decides the way in which all men must work. As he himself explained it, only those who work with him gather, while the rest scatter only. (Luke 11:23.)

4. But this testimony to the activity of God in judgment, of which Jesus Christ is the judge, because he is God's intervention in and God's decision for human life, is set within the context of the promise that Jesus is *he through whom all things fulfill their destiny.*

In the prophecy of Jeremiah the new beginning is set out

in these terms: "I will put my law within them, and I will write it upon their hearts; . . . for I will forgive their iniquity, and I will remember their sin no more" (Jer. 31:33-34). A great act of forgiveness is the matrix within which judgment is exercised: or, in New Testament terms, Christ's act of atonement forms also the basis of the judgment he exercises.

The New Testament does not worry about the logical contradiction between its teaching that damnation is a possibility for men, so that this may be the judgment which is pronounced on some at the last, and its teaching that God's plan in Christ for the fullness of time is to unite all things in him. (Eph. 1:10.) Indeed, the New Testament shows that it is out of this very contradiction that there arises both the gospel which is proclaimed and the reason for proclaiming it. If salvation is by grace, damnation cannot be by works: so that the issue of faith and unfaith must be stringently understood in relation to the person and work of Jesus Christ.

This recapitulation, however, of all things in Jesus Christ, at the end of the process of history, is already taking place in the world. It is personal experience that when the entries in the book of men's lives are brought under the heading of Jesus Christ, many a transaction which seemed at the time to be gain will be seen really to have been loss, while others which seemed at the time to have been loss will be seen to be gain. Besides, because this life and activity of Jesus Christ is his life and activity in the world, it is meaningful to speak too of human cultures being recapitulated in him and through him. Thus, when an Indian thinker speaks of "wedding the Spirit of Christ with the spirit of India," he is asking that Christ's presence in India be discerned so that that which belongs to India may be brought into his obedience and into the service of his glory. "They shall bring [unto Zion] the glory and the honor of the nations." (Rev. 21:26.)

5. The climax of the biblical testimony, therefore, to the finality of Jesus Christ is that it is *he unto whom all things go.* This is the natural climax to the affirmation that the finality of Jesus Christ is not simply the finality of himself as a person, but is also the finality of his work as the effective presence in the world of the kingdom and reign of God.

On the one hand, there is this reign as it impinges on human life through the exercise of Christ's Lordship and Saviorhood. On the other hand, there is the work of the Holy Spirit in the hearts and minds of men, evoking repentance and faith, and enabling the response of obedience and discipleship. The finality of Jesus Christ receives its full trinitarian affirmation only as it takes seriously this New Testament witness to the work of the Holy Spirit. For apart from him the gift of grace in Jesus Christ is not received. It is the Holy Spirit who teaches men to live by the Father's welcome, enabling each man to say, "Abba"—"my Father." It is also by him that they are led to inherit that which Jesus Christ has made their inheritance. (Rom. 8:16-17.)

This essential work of Christ and the Holy Spirit has as its center the way in which things and persons are brought by them to participation in the crisis of Christ's death and resurrection. Individuals die with him in his death and find that in losing themselves they save themselves. Also, every perception of truth and every system of moral behavior is brought to dissolution by him, when it is submitted to him, and then resurrected to new life within his obedience and in his service.

The finality of Jesus Christ, as the Bible declares it, however, does not consist only in the finality of the Person and his work. It also consists in the finality of the witness borne to him. The community which carries his name bears this finality as a mark of its life.

When Scripture works out the relation between the universal and the particular in the structure of Christian faith, it also includes in its teaching the way in which this relation is exemplified in the reality of the church—that is, in the relation between the purposes of God for the whole of creation and the work of God in the community of witness. This is why the Christian community is compared to the first fruits of a harvest. The first fruits are the guarantee of the whole harvest and part of it. As James has it, "Of his own will he brought us forth by the word of truth that we should be a kind of first fruits of his creatures" (James 1:18). The call and the blessing of Abraham, which is the first act in the story of how the whole human community took particular form in a people bearing God's name, has this relation between the universal and the particular explicitly stated in the call itself. "I will bless . . . you, . . . and by you all the families of the earth will bless themselves." (Gen. 12:3.)

How does this happen? The answer given, on the one hand, is to speak of the representative nature of Christ and, on the other hand, to speak of the way in which the church participates in that nature. In his letter to the Hebrews the writer says, "As it is, we do not yet see everything in subjection to [man]. But we see Jesus" (Heb. 2:8-9). The thrust of the verse is not that that which is not yet will be accomplished because of what has already happened in and to Jesus Christ, but that what has happened in and to Jesus Christ is already the end, the end toward which all things are set. "We . . . grow, . . ." says Paul, "into him who is the head, into Christ" (Eph. 4:15).

Jesus Christ is representative man. That which happened to him happened to all humanity, so that it is this happening which is then unfolded through the process of time. The passage in Daniel (Dan. 7:13-14) to which the verse in Hebrews alludes, speaks of the Son of man. The Son of man is man in his divine human-ness. He is what God intended man to be. When

25

Jesus chose this title for himself (Matt. 16:13), this was the claim that he was making. "I am man." And, when his disciples called him the Son of God (Matt. 16:16), that was their way of accepting his claim. For the Son of man is Son of man only because he is the Son of God. He is God's decisive deed on man's behalf. He is for man his new beginning. In him all humanity is represented.

Also, since there is only one name by which men can be saved (Acts 4:12), only one way to the Father (John 14:6), therefore in him all must meet. If there are many ways for men to attain their destiny, they can go by those several ways without meeting one another. But if there is only one way and one door, all men must meet. The human community is constituted by the finality of Jesus Christ. All things are not only from him, but unto him.

In this representativeness of Christ the church shares, because not only are all things set toward him, but he himself who is the end has happened to the church. In Paul's words the church is that on which "the end of the ages has come" (I Cor. 10:11). It is that for which tomorrow is over. In describing the Christian life both John and Paul use violent metaphors. John speaks of a second birth (John 3:3), while Paul speaks of a death and resurrection (Rom. 6:3-4). There is one thing certain about every child when it is born—it will die. Paul makes the claim that, for the Christian, this certain event is over. He has already died. The death he will die some day is only the physical counterpart of a death he has died already. That is why death has no sting and the grave no victory. (I Cor. 15:55.) The life of the church is this resurrected life. "Destroy this temple," Jesus said, "and . . . I will raise it up" (John 2:19). John adds the comment, "He spoke of the temple of his body" (John 2:21).

How many Christians live as those for whom death is over?

26

What will it mean to do so? It will mean, will it not, that when they do something well they will be able to forget it and not be disappointed if no one gives them credit for it. They will know what it is to have the signature of death written across all their achievements, just as it has been written across all their sins. How many (and here I am talking about Ceylon) profess that they are prepared to carry the cross for Jesus' sake, but decide to emigrate if they are overlooked for a promotion on the ground that they are Christians! No, it cannot be said of most of us that we are dead. We are very much alive to what we think the world owes us. The Christian practice of death means nothing more and nothing less than allowing people to treat us as they treated Jesus himself. When Paul said, I am dead, but Christ is alive in me (Gal. 2:20), he was saying, You can deal with me as you dealt with Jesus Christ. That is the crux of the Christian calling. "Are you able," Jesus asks, "to drink the cup that I drink, or to be baptized with the baptism with which I am baptized?" (Mark 10:38).

The other side of this truth is that not only is death over but the resurrection is over, too. He who is risen is already the Lord. And yet, how little acknowledgment is made of this lordship. There is too great a readiness to harbor grievances, to press claims, to ask for recognition, as if the final reality is not the lordship of Christ but the freedom of men. It is true, is it not, that as far as any man is concerned, he is not at another man's mercy, not even his own, for Christ is already Lord of all men and all things.

But it is not only in this personal dimension that witness is borne to the finality of Christ: for it has this implication, too, that those who so witness are committed by the witness they bear both to believe in the presence of Jesus Christ in the history of all other faiths, as well as to accept their responsibility to declare to men of other faiths the identity of "the unknown

27

God" by whom each man's faith is validated and their systems of faith are judged. (Acts 17:23.)

To disclose the "unknown God" is not to rename the known gods. Instead, it is to uncover a presence which has been there even though unidentified: indeed, a presence that was forgotten and lost, if not denied. To put the matter in another way, the known gods represent the past tense in one's religious history. It is the present tense, the way in which God is contemporarily present, which needs to be discerned and named. That this present tense has always been present is what makes the name of Jesus appropriate for it.

This witness to the unknown God rests, too, on another fact: that when Jesus Christ makes his place and time of appointment with men, he does not always give his name. I can imagine a man such as Jawaharlal Nehru saying, "But when did I see you naked or hungry or in prison?" (Matt. 25:37-39). The point is not that there are alternatives to commitment to Christ, other ways by which men can be saved; but that to speak about the finality of Christ is not to tie oneself to where his name is actually pronounced. As he himself tells us, he determines the form and occasion of his presence, and where and to whom he will come incognito. Also, is it not the converse of this fact that he is emphasizing when he says that if the son who has said "Yes" will not obey, then the father will win his obedience from the son who says "No" (Matt. 21:28-31)?

To fulfill, then, the Christian responsibility with regard to other faiths and their adherents, Christians must, as it were, be prepared to engage simultaneously in three dialogues. First, there will be the inner dialogue through which their own faith in Jesus Christ is matured and fructified by the testimony of other men to God's ways with them. The Christian must never forget that he is always as one who sees baffling reflections in a mirror (I Cor. 13:12), and that others constantly make clear to him many things which he finds perplexing. Secondly, there will be the outer dialogue in which Christians and those who are not engage each other in conversation. The intent of this dialogue is to discern the ways of God in each other's religion and religious experience—in the questions that are asked, the search which is conducted, and the answers found. For nowhere has God left himself without witness. (Acts 14:17.) Also, since Jesus Christ and the Holy Spirit are at work in the lives of all men, each man is at a particular moment in Jesus Christ. It is this moment, with respect to each, which needs to be discerned, so that the dialogue may take place in the company of Jesus. And finally, there is the essential dialogue between each man and Jesus Christ in which, as it were, those in outer dialogue stand by one another silently, upholding one another in mutual concern. The culmination of this essential dialogue for all men has to be their conversion to Jesus Christ—him with whom they must die and by and for whom they must live. The witness of the Christian to the finality of Jesus Christ is a witness through and within all these three dialogues.

But Christian witness to the finality of Jesus Christ has a third implication also: for there is the witness to be borne together by those who bear his name. The issues concerning church union have their own inherent difficulty. This is no place to talk about them. Nevertheless, it is essential to remember here that no one may talk about the finality of Christ and, at the same time, remain careless of the necessity of all those who bear his name belonging to one family and living a common family life. Jesus Christ must be sufficient for his people, both to unite them and to enable them to be enriched by their differences. The tragedy of denominations is that they are an attempt to organize dogmatic differences, to give to "the baffling reflections" institutional and structural expression. The finality of Jesus Christ is a standing judgment on denominational separateness. He is enough; he alone must be enough.

The church cannot fulfill its role as the home of the human dialogue, the dialogue between man and man and between man and God, if it does not in its own life sustain that dialogue. It is the foundation of the church which is fixed; its walls on every side must have open gates through which the traffic of life can flow. To close these gates against fellow Christian or fellow man is to deny the nature of the church.

We have referred already to two basic differences in the structure of faith as between Christianity and other religions. We have seen that the coordinates within which the graph of the Christian faith was plotted were determined by the relation between the universal and the particular as this relation is in Jesus Christ, and also by the this-worldliness which the coming of Jesus Christ signifies and to which it gives effect. We can state now the third factor which constitutes this difference: that whereas in all other religions and systems of belief the present is determined by the past, in Christianity the present is determined by the future. It is to this difference that the Christian community bears witness by the eschatological nature of its existence.

An integral part of the good news of the gospel is in this fact that the future is over, and that the history of man is not something that is being pushed from behind but is something that is being pulled from in front. Indeed, this witness to an accomplished future toward which all things are set is part of the biblical testimony to the transcendence of God. Here is the reason for that intractability and intransigence with which men find they have to deal, both in their personal lives and behavior and in their life together as communities. Whenever Scripture speaks about predestination, it is about the destination that it speaks. It is the destination which has been determined.

To believe that today is determined by yesterday is to believe in salvation by works, whereas to believe that today is determined by tomorrow is to believe in salvation by grace. Yesterday is over, yes; but tomorrow is over, too. He who will be crowned Lord is Lord already. He who will come to judge is already engaged in judgment. The final consummation is already the end toward which all things are set. The fruits of men's labor are already the gifts of his love.

"Jesus, knowing that . . . he had come from God and was going to God . . . girded himself with a towel." (John 13:3-4.)

# 2

## THE CHRISTOLOGY OF THE
## NEW TESTAMENT
## JESUS AND THE SON OF MAN

The Christology of the New Testament cannot, of course, be fully and adequately treated in one chapter. Nor is the subject of this chapter in any way limited by the title, "The Finality of Christ." For what else is the entire New Testament about except precisely the finality of Christ?—whether it is expressed in Johannine terms of the Logos which was before creation and is now made flesh; or in the terminology of Hebrews, which contrasts the preparation of the Old Testament era and the activity of God in these last days; or in the magnificent language of Ephesians, which sees Christ exalted to sit in heavenly places at the right hand of God; or in the "simple" message of the gospels, where the dawning kingdom of God (and this remains true whatever breed of eschatology one favors) is closely connected with the person and preaching of Jesus. Faced with this situation, one must choose one aspect of the theme, and I have rashly ventured to choose that of the Son of man—though once again, one needs a book to do justice to the subject.[1] But I choose it for two reasons: (a) be-

---

[1] I hope shortly to publish a more detailed examination of this subject.

cause, if the Gospels are to be believed, this is the term which Jesus himself used of himself: here, if anywhere, we are in touch with his own understanding of his finality, and it therefore seems appropriate to use it as the focus of our study; (b) because I suspect that the ideas with which it is associated underlie much of the rest of the New Testament, even though they are expressed elsewhere in different terms.

# I

The traditional belief that Jesus spoke of himself in terms of the Son of man has recently been under the strongest attack. The view of Rudolf Bultmann,[2] that Jesus spoke of another as Son of man, once regarded as extreme, is now almost orthodoxy on the continent; recent supporters of this view are John Knox[3] and A. J. B. Higgins.[4] Such is the change in the climate of thought, that when I ventured to support the more traditional view recently, I was told by one Swiss scholar that my views were "revolutionary!" Bultmann's views are no longer regarded as radical; in the opinion of some scholars—e.g., Vielhauer[5] and Conzelmann[6]—he has not gone far enough. In their view Jesus never used the term "Son of man" at all, whether of himself or another, and its presence in the Gospels is due entirely to the early church. I do not myself believe that the evidence of the Gospels supports this view, but these scholars have laid a finger on one of the fundamental weaknesses of

[2] E.g., *Theology of the New Testament*, Kendrick Grobel, tr., I (New York: Charles Scribner's Sons, 1951), 26-32.

[3] *The Death of Christ* (Nashville: Abingdon Press, 1958), pp. 52-109.

[4] *Jesus and the Son of Man* (Philadelphia: Fortress Press, 1965).

[5] "Gottesreich und Menschensohn in der Verkündigung Jesu," *Festschrift für Günther Dehn*, W. Schneemelcher, ed. (Neukirchen: Kreis Moers, 1957), pp. 51-79.

[6] "Gegenwart und Zukunft in der synoptischen Tradition," *Zeitschrift für Theologie und Kirche* (Tübingen, 1957), pp. 277-96.

Bultmann's and Knox's position: the role of Jesus himself.[7] If, as all these scholars believe, Jesus himself stood in a particular relation to the coming kingdom, then what room is there for another who is Son of man? For this relationship in itself seems to imply some kind of "finality" for Jesus; he is more than simply one who announces the kingdom's coming. If, on the other hand, he spoke of another as the coming Son of man, who is to be the eschatological Judge, then what is the role of Jesus himself? Is he only the penultimate figure? It is this apparent contradiction between sayings about the kingdom and sayings about the Son of man which causes some scholars to solve the problem by attributing the former tradition to Jesus and the latter to the church, and viewing them as two different ways of expressing the finality of Christ.

For the majority of Christians the mind of Jesus himself— how he thought of himself and the terms which he used of himself—is all-important. Their attitude can be summed up in the words of J. W. Bowman: *"The Church cannot indefinitely continue to believe about Jesus what he did not know to be true about himself!"* [8] This declaration raises important questions for Christology which I cannot deal with now; I simply note here that its assumptions have been challenged recently by John Knox.[9] But whatever our attitude to this problem, the question, "Did Jesus think and speak of himself as the Son of man or not?" remains an important one. Possibly even more important is the question: "What did those who first identified Jesus with the Son of man—whether it was Jesus himself or the early church—mean by this term?" I believe that the answer to *this* question may perhaps provide also the answer to the ques-

[7] *Ibid.*, pp. 281-82.
[8] *The Intention of Jesus* (Philadelphia: The Westminster Press, 1943), p. 121.
[9] *The Death of Christ*, pp. 33-51.

tion: "Did Jesus use the term of himself?" For the attack on the old traditional view has been made on the grounds that the self-identification of Jesus with the Son of man is psychologically incredible, and that form-criticism has unraveled the process by which the strange hodgepodge of "Son of man" sayings were attributed to Jesus. Any defense of the traditional view, therefore, must convince us, firstly, that the self-identification of Jesus with the Son of man *is psychologically* credible, and, secondly, that the "Son of man" material in the gospels is perhaps more coherent than has often been supposed. It is my purpose in this chapter to suggest that an examination of the background of the term reveals such a coherent pattern.

We must begin in the Old Testament, and I make no apology for doing so; we can never understand the New Testament without it—least of all on a subject such as the finality of Christ. In this particular case I believe it to be of especial importance, because the Old Testament and intertestamental evidence seem to be at variance with the assumptions which many scholars make about the term "Son of man" in the Gospels. I turn first to Daniel 7.

## II

If we are going to understand the significance of the figure "like a Son of man" in Daniel 7, then it is essential to consider it in relation to the background of the book and not to isolate it from the rest of what Daniel has to say. There is a tendency to separate the description of the one like a Son of man from the rest of Daniel's message, and to speak of the glorious Son of man without much reference to the rest of the book, or even the rest of the chapter. This approach leads, I believe, to a misunderstanding both of Daniel's purpose and of the Son of man.

The background against which the book of Daniel was written was a desperate one; the situation can be summed up in the three words—war, occupation, and martyrdom. The outlook for the Jewish faith could not have been more grim. God seemed to have abandoned his people, and those who were faithful to him and to his Law were the ones who suffered. It is in this situation that the author of the book of Daniel attempted to write a message of encouragement and comfort to the faithful remnant in Israel, urging them to remain true to their faith and to the Law. Although at the moment things could not look blacker, yet he urges them to hang on, because eventually everything is going to be all right. It is this basic situation and message of hope which is depicted in chapter 7 in pictorial language. The enemies which have oppressed and overrun Israel are depicted as wild animals; the Ancient of Days then sits in judgment, and Daniel watches while the fourth and most terrible beast is slain; finally, one like a Son of man is brought to stand before the Ancient of Days and is given authority and glory and rule.

The fact that the phrase "Son of man" is used in Dan. 7:13 as a comparison suggests that, whatever else this figure may or may not be, he is not a mere Son of man, any more than the beast which is described in verse 6 as "like a leopard, with four wings of a bird on its back; and . . . four heads" is to be understood as a mere leopard. What, then, is he? One popular explanation is that the origin of Daniel's figure is to be found in that of the Urmensch. Various scholars have endeavored to trace the "one like a Son of man" to some form of the idea of a primal or heavenly man, and the attempt is justified, in so far as both belong ultimately to the same mythological pattern of thought. But it is very doubtful whether the Urmensch helps us in understanding the figure "like a Son of man" in Daniel. Even if the author did have such a heavenly being in mind, the ideas which he borrowed have been so radically changed in his use of them that it is doubtful whether they could have been of any great significance to him, and even more doubtful whether they would have conveyed any particular significance to his readers. His concern—and theirs—is not with a heavenly man, but with the fortunes of Israel.

The pattern of the vision in Daniel 7 has been shaped by the primitive myth of creation; the emergence of the beasts from the sea, their defeat by Yahweh, and the bestowal of dominion on a human figure, are all motifs taken from this background. Creation mythology played a central role in the Babylonian cultus, and it is possible that Daniel has borrowed traits from her tradition. Far more significant, however, is the fact that a similar pattern of thought was already an integral part of Hebrew religion; Daniel is not introducing ideas which were alien to the Hebrew tradition. His affinity with earlier Hebraic thought is illustrated by the character in which he portrays the beasts: they are still the powers of chaos, revolting against God's rule, but now they are no longer natural forces but nations. In depicting Israel's enemies as wild beasts, Daniel is following the tradition of prophets and psalmists, who often described hostile nations in these unflattering terms.[10]

We can trace in the Old Testament two distinct but interwoven themes: one is the conflict between Israel and her enemies, represented as wild beasts; the other is the conquest of chaos by Yahweh. The relationship between these two themes is plain: Yahweh's struggle with the monster is parallel with the nation's battle with her enemies, and it is God's victory which ensures the well-being of the people. In the Babylonian ritual the two themes seem to have coalesced, for the king played the role of the god in the battle with Tiamat. But

[10] E.g., Ps. 68:30; 74:18-19; Ezek. 29:3-4.

in the Hebrew prophets, though the themes may be parallel, they are not identical. For while the powers of chaos may be reinterpreted in terms of Israel's enemies, Yahweh and the nation or its king remain distinct. Thus the emphasis is upon Yahweh as active and triumphant, working for the salvation of his people, and upon the nation as saved from the power of her enemies; the relationship is a three-cornered one, involving Yahweh, Israel, and her enemies.

Now it is precisely this three-cornered relationship which reappears in Daniel's vision. For the first decisive event takes place between the Ancient of Days and the rebellious beasts, and does not involve the one like a Son of man at all. Judgment is given, the forces of chaos are crushed, and the fourth beast is slain. Only at this point does the Son of man arrive before the throne of judgment. He is, in fact, a curiously inactive figure—no heavenly Redeemer this, but simply the recipient of God's mercy and salvation, as Israel has always been. To this human figure the Ancient of Days gives the kingdom which has been usurped by the rebellious forces of chaos.

Now the point of Daniel's imagery here lies, I believe, in the Jewish belief that Israel was the chosen nation of the Lord and in the way in which that belief was often expressed in contemporary literature. In some of the apocryphal and pseudepigraphal writings, we find the idea that Israel, as the chosen nation, is the inheritor of the promises which were made to Adam. The authority and dominion which were given to Adam at the creation were meant also for his descendants—not, however, for mankind in general, but for Israel. As for the rest of the nations, they are not recognized as true descendants of Adam; on the contrary, they are often depicted as the beasts, who have usurped the authority and rule which by rights belong to Israel. Typical is this passage from II Esdras 6 in which the author complains about God's inactivity:

38

On the sixth day thou didst command the earth to bring forth
before thee cattle, beasts, and creeping things; and over these thou
didst place Adam, as ruler over all the works which thou hadst
made; and from him we have all come, the people whom thou hast
chosen.

All this I have spoken before thee, O Lord, because thou hast
said that it was for us that thou didst create this world. As for the
other nations which have descended from Adam, thou hast said
that they are nothing, and that they are like spittle, and thou hast
compared their abundance to a drop from a bucket. And now, O
Lord, behold, these nations, which are reputed as nothing, domineer
over us and devour us. But we thy people, whom thou hast called
thy first-born, only begotten, zealous for thee, and most dear, have
been given into their hands. If the world has indeed been created
for us, why do we not possess our world as an inheritance? How
long will this be so?

When, in his vision, Daniel depicts Israel's enemies as
beasts, and Israel herself as one like a Son of man, he is expressing this same belief that Israel is the inheritor of the
promise made to Adam, whose authority has been usurped by
the other nations. His vision is a prophecy of what he believes
will shortly take place upon the earth. Restoration is at hand;
as in the old mythology the beast is slain by Yahweh, and
dominion is given to man, so now, those who are like beasts
are to be conquered, and dominion is to be given to the one like
a Son of man. In other words, Daniel's vision is an assurance to
Israel that the purposes of God have not failed and will not
fail; Israel is the one like a Son of man, the inheritor of the
promises made to Adam, who is intended by God to rule the
world. In spite of the fact that at the moment other nations
have usurped the power and dominion which belong by right
to Israel, they will be overthrown by God himself, who will
restore the kingdom to Israel.

All this is, of course, typically nationalistic. But we should notice the other side of the picture. Adam lost his authority and dominion in the world because he was disobedient to God, and Israel will only be given back this authority and dominion if she is obedient to God. Obedience and authority go together. It is not Israel as a whole to whom dominion and glory are promised, but the saints of the Most High—those who are obedient to God and faithful to the Law. It is to those who fulfill the will of God that Daniel can confidently promise authority and glory and dominion.

The beasts and the human figure in Daniel are not, then, mere symbols which disguise the real characters in the drama. His vision is not simply a fanciful and pictorial representation of a pious hope that everything will come right in the end, but a revelation which conveys a message of real significance to a tortured people. Daniel offers a message of hope. But it is important to notice the basis of this hope. It is *not*, as is so often said, a hope that Israel will one day *become* the Son of man, and so be given glory, dominion, and authority. Rather, it is precisely because Israel is now the Son of man, that Daniel can confidently promise a glorious future; these things will come to Israel because they are Israel's right, as the inheritor of the promises of God. Although not recognized as such, Israel *is* the Son of man to whom the kingdom belongs. This is why Daniel can say to the faithful nucleus of the nation: Cheer up! If you are faithful to God and stand firm, then he will be faithful to *his* promise to give you the earth and dominion over it. At the moment other nations do not recognize either God's authority or yours, and so you are suffering, but eventually God will intervene, and you will be given the glory and rule intended for you.

And so we find that the paradox of the suffering Son of man is an integral part of Daniel's vision. It is a paradox, because

40

the Son of man is meant to exercise authority over others; but at the moment that authority is not recognized, and the saints are suffering.

The evidence of Daniel does not, then, support Sigmund Mowinckel, when he writes:

> We can conclude from Dan. vii that about 200 B.C. or earlier there was in Judaism a conception of a heavenly being in human form who, at the turn of the age, the dawn of the eschatological era, would appear, and would receive from God delegated power and authority over all kingdoms and peoples.[11]

Neither the material used by Daniel nor the interpretation which he gives to it, supports the view that such a heavenly being was known in Judaism at that time.

But what of the time of Christ two centuries later? Has the Son of man by this time become a heavenly eschatological figure? According to I Enoch, at least, the answer is "Yes." The author has interpreted the symbols of Dan. 7:13 literally, and the Son of man is now an eschatological figure exercising judgment over the kings of the earth; he is both an individual and a heavenly being. Yet it is perhaps as well to remember that he is not entirely individualized—nor, indeed, entirely heavenly. Though no longer corporate, the Son of man retains vestiges of his corporate nature. As leader of the elect community, he is closely associated with his followers; he can, indeed, be described as a prototype of Mary with her little lamb, for wherever the Righteous and Elect One goes, there, sure enough, the little righteous and elect ones go, too. And though now an exalted figure, his feet are not entirely off the ground and on

[11] *He That Cometh*, G. W. Anderson, tr. (Nashville: Abingdon Press, 1956), p. 352; italics mine.

41

the clouds, for at the end of the Similitudes he turns out to be none other than the humble, righteous Enoch.

By the time we get to II Esdras, however, at the end of the first century A.D., the Son of man has become a true eschatological figure who rises from the sea and hovers in the clouds and lands on mountaintops, like some giant eschatological helicopter.

# III

I have already referred to the psychological difficulties which some scholars feel in supposing that Jesus identified himself with the Son of man. This point of view has been put most ably and persuasively by John Knox: "How could [so sane a person] have identified himself with the essentially superhuman personage of the apocalypses—with him who, 'sitting at the right hand of Power,' will come 'with the clouds of heaven'?" [12]

Now the point of Knox's difficulty is that he finds it impossible to think of a sane man identifying himself with an eschatological supernatural figure sitting on the clouds. But are we sure that, when Jesus spoke of the Son of man, he was necessarily thinking of this eschatological cloud-borne figure? Knox and Bultmann are, and for that very reason they have eliminated any other kind of "Son of man" saying (e.g., the predictions of suffering) from the discussion. But is there perhaps not a flaw in the argument here? They begin their examination with the belief that the Son of man is an eschatological figure, eliminate all the "Son of man" sayings in the Gospel tradition which do not fit that eschatological picture, and then complain that they find the remaining evidence, on its own, incredible. I suggest that this procedure is only justified if we

[12] *The Death of Christ*, p. 58.

are certain that "the Son of man" was necessarily and exclusively interpreted at the time of Jesus as meaning "the eschatological redeemer who is going to appear at the end of the time riding upon clouds."

Now at first sight the evidence seems to support this kind of interpretation. For the Gospels seem to point firmly to Daniel 7 as the source of the sayings in the mouth of Jesus, and the reference there is to the Son of man coming in the clouds. The only explanations of Daniel 7 which we have (in I Enoch and II Esdras) both understand the term "Son of man" in this way. And the largest group of Son of man sayings can be classified as eschatological. Nevertheless, I do not believe that this evidence *does* support the idea that "the Son of man" is a kind of shorthand for "the eschatological redeemer who rides on the clouds."

1) The evidence of Daniel does not support it, for in Daniel the one like a Son of man represents Israel, and the vision is not meant to be taken literally. The author does *not* expect an eschatological redeemer to appear on clouds at the end of the world; he expects the saints in Israel to be vindicated by God. Obviously this does not necessarily mean that Jesus (if he used the term) applied it in the same sense; but it does leave the possibility open that he, too, used it symbolically rather than interpreting the details literally.

2) The evidence of I Enoch and II Esdras does not support it. Certainly, they indicate that in some circles the vision of the Son of man was interpreted literally. But we do not know how widespread this interpretation was. There is no other evidence for this approach; was it the normal interpretation of Daniel 7 during the first half of the first century A.D.? I Enoch is of uncertain date; II Esdras was certainly not yet written. Moreover, II Esdras interprets the details of Daniel's vision in a more crude and literal sense than Enoch, and this suggests

43

that this kind of understanding was still developing after the time of Jesus.

3) The Gospel evidence does not support it. We have a considerable number of sayings in which "the Son of man" quite clearly does *not* mean "the eschatological redeemer coming on the clouds." In order to support the view of Bultmann and Knox, we must regard these other sayings as inventions of the early church. The explanation given is that the church made two mistakes: (a) it falsely assumed that when Jesus used the term "Son of man" he was referring to himself, not to another, and so it came to identify him with the Son of man; (b) it concluded that Jesus commonly used the term "Son of man" to designate himself where he might well have said "I," and so it incorrectly inserted the term in inappropriate contexts. But there are grave difficulties with this explanation: (a) This development all happened very quickly—during the Aramaic-speaking period of the church. Was there time for *both* these steps to be taken? (b) For Bultmann and Knox "the Son of man" is a symbol for "the eschatological redeemer coming on the clouds"; *this* is what makes Jesus' use of the term as a self-designation incredible. But *if* "Son of man" is shorthand for "eschatological redeemer coming on the clouds," how did the church—at such an early stage—come to use the term in these other contexts where, *ex hypothesi*, it so obviously did not fit? The fact that the church so quickly, according to Bultmann and Knox, forgot the "real eschatological meaning" of the term, suggests that it was not quite so eschatological and supernatural as they suppose. (c) There is a tendency in the Gospel tradition to develop and emphasize the apocalyptic and eschatological element in the "Son of man" sayings. If there is a development *toward* the eschatological interpretation, does not this suggest that the "original" Son of man in the Gospels may in fact have been *less* supernatural than now

44

appears? May it not be a distortion of the evidence, then, to eliminate this other, noneschatological element altogether? (d) Was the early church quite so ready to put Christological terms into the mouth of Jesus as is supposed? A comparison with the term "Christ" suggests not. Certainly "Christ" is found occasionally in the words of Jesus in the Gospels and may well have been put there by the early church. But there is a marked contrast between the scanty references to Christ in the Gospels, and the large number of references to the Son of man, as also between the vast number of references to Christ in the rest of the New Testament, and the almost complete absence of references to the Son of man.

The Son of man whom Knox finds a psychological stumbling block is a figure built up out of part of the evidence. In his approach he has followed the method which is almost invariably used by those who tackle this problem. The first step is to divide the sayings into various groups—usually three: the "eschatological," the "suffering," and the "general." The next step is to eliminate one, two, or even three of these groups from the discussion. One reason for this method is that it is very difficult to see how the three groups hang together. It is easier to present a coherent picture with only two of them, even easier with only one. So we find even C. E. B. Cranfield,[13] who does not normally eliminate sayings from the Gospels, prepared to sacrifice one group for this reason.

Nevertheless, to bulldoze a third or even two thirds of the evidence in this way is a highly dangerous procedure. If we cannot see how the strands of tradition belong together, may it perhaps not be because we have the wrong ideas about the Son of man? If three strands of string are twisted together to

[13] *The Gospel According to Saint Mark* (Cambridge: Cambridge University Press, 1959), pp. 100, 117-18.

make a rope, it is obviously a foolish procedure to divide them, extract one, and say "this is the real rope." May it not be that the three strands of tradition in the Gospels together represent the truth about the Son of man? That perhaps the church has got them all slightly tangled? And that we, in trying to pull the strands apart and separate them, have only added to the confusion? When Higgins, e.g., dismissses the "Son of man" sayings from the discussion one by one on the grounds that they are "inauthentic," may he not be simplifying the issue?

## IV

I should like to illustrate this by looking at the total picture presented by Mark. I choose his gospel because it is the earliest and because the pattern of Son of man sayings is seen there most clearly. Obviously such a choice is open to the criticism that the picture which emerges may be Mark's own, but the same pattern can, I believe, be found elsewhere. Let us begin with the "eschatological" sayings. Here we have Knox's "supernatural redeemer on the clouds of heaven." Or have we? Certainly we have clouds, in 13:26 and 14:62, and glory, in 8:38 and 13:26. And certainly Mark seems to have understood the clouds literally. But did Jesus? Did Jesus really foretell the arrival of a supernatural Son of man to exercise judgment on the earth? Or did he, like the author of Daniel, intend his language to be understood symbolically? The fact that his quotations are taken from Daniel suggests that we should at least consider the possibility that he is using Daniel's language in Daniel's way. It seems to me significant that all three of these sayings appear in a context where they stand in contrast to the present suffering of Jesus and his followers. The irony of the paradoxical situation is seen in the trial scene: the Son of man has been handed over into the power of men, who do with him what they want: nevertheless, his vindication is at hand: very soon he will "come" on the clouds of heaven, and sit at the right hand of God: not only will the human judgment be reversed, but the Son of man will be given a position of authority. In Mark 8:38, the vindication or condemnation is of those who follow him or have been ashamed of him: the Son of man exercises judgment. Mark 13:26 is rejected by almost all commentators as sheer apocalyptic. It would be rash indeed to build on that chapter. Yet it is worth noting that the saying about the Son of man appears in the same kind of context: after the trials and tribulations of Jesus' followers, their sufferings are ended by the advent of the Son of man: for them, this event means vindication and the reversal of their former fortunes.

Is it accidental that Mark links the coming of the Son of man with the sufferings of the faithful (as in Daniel), rather than dwelling on the details of the judgment (as in I Enoch)?

But whether we take these "Son of man" sayings symbolically or literally, there is no denying that their basic reference is to the future authority of the Son of man. Whoever or whatever he is, the Son of man is intended to exercise authority in future, and, as in Daniel, to receive dominion and judgment.

But what of the *suffering* Son of man? There are two popular ways of dealing with these sayings. One is to add the idea of the Servant. The other is to subtract the term "Son of man." The first is popular with British commentators who believe that Jesus combined the title "Son of man" with the concept of the Servant;[14] the second is adopted by those scholars who believe that these sayings reflect the dogma of the early church. Neither solution answers the problem. Why does the tradition here preserve the title "Son of man"? For this

---

[14] I have discussed this view in *Jesus and the Servant* (London: S. P. C. K., 1959).

group of sayings presents us with the belief that it was as Son of man that Jesus suffered. Can it perhaps be that it was precisely because he was Son of man that he suffered?

At first sight the suggestion that the idea of the Son of man itself necessarily includes that of suffering may seem absurd: he is a figure naturally associated with glory. It is true that the saints in Daniel 7 suffer, but this suffering is not a necessary attribute of the Son of man—quite the reverse; it is something which ought not to happen. At this point, however, we may perhaps approach the problem in a different way and ask, not "Why must the Son of man suffer?" but "How can the Son of man suffer?" If we turn again to Daniel, the answer to this question is immediately clear: the Son of man can—and will—suffer when his rightful position and God's authority are denied. This is the situation in Daniel 7, where the "beasts" have revolted against God and have crushed Israel who, as Son of man, should be ruling the earth with the authority granted by God. Given this situation of the nations' revolt and their rejection of the claims of the one who is intended to exercise authority, it is true to say that the Son of man not only can but must suffer. Similarly, in II Esdras, Israel suffers, although destined to be Adam's heir, because the other nations have seized power and denied Israel the inheritance: the nation will be released from suffering and take over the rule, only when the other nations are subdued and recognize Israel's authority.

If we return now to the sayings in Mark and ask how the Son of man there can suffer, then the answer will be the same. He can—and will—suffer if men set themselves up against God and reject the claims of the one to whom he has given authority. In this situation the suffering of the Son of man is inevitable, and the suffering will end only when his authority is recognized and accepted. This, however, is precisely the situation which, according to Mark, already exists. The rejection of

Jesus by the authorities is described in these sayings as a future necessity, but the necessity arises from the fact that the rejection has already taken place; scribes and Pharisees have already refused to accept the claim of the Son of man to God-given authority; Pharisees and Herodians have already plotted together to kill him. The authority of the Son of man has been repeatedly demonstrated and repeatedly rejected, and, unless and until the powers which have set themselves up in opposition to God are finally overthrown, suffering is inevitable. The suffering of the Son of man results from the opposition of the beast, who represents rebellion against the authority of God. This is the theme which underlies the whole gospel: the suffering and death of Jesus, like the whole of his ministry, represent a conflict with the satanic forces of evil and rebellion against God.

There is, then, a close and essential link between the authority of Jesus and his rejection, between his Messiahship and his suffering. It is for this reason, I suggest, that the teaching about the passion is so closely linked with the confession at Caesarea Philippi. It is only to those men who accept his authority that Jesus can explain the necessity and inevitability of his suffering, for the one arises, paradoxically, out of the other. When authority is rejected, suffering must follow.

These two groups of sayings about the Son of man represent two aspects of his authority. We see what happens when that authority is rejected, and what will happen when that authority is finally established. But what of that third group of "Son of man" sayings, of which we have two examples in Mark, which refer to the Son of man without mentioning either suffering or glory? Now commentators are generally very unhappy with these two sayings. Those who believe that Jesus spoke only of a future, glorious Son of man, obviously regard references to the Son of man here as an anachronism introduced by the early church; but many of those who think that Jesus spoke also of a suffering Son of man can find no link between these two passages and their understanding of the term "Son of man."

Support for this view that the sayings come from the early church is often found in the fact that these two sayings stand alone in splendid isolation from the rest of the "Son of man" sayings, not only in their content, but in context, too. Six chapters separate them from the rest of the sayings, which all occur after Caesarea Philippi. This fact leads Cranfield, e.g., to suspect 2:28. He writes: "Would Jesus have used the term thus openly at this stage of his ministry and in conversation with his opponents?" [15] Now this argument is really rather curious. For the *position* of an incident in Mark can tell us something about the probable genuineness of its contents only if we can fix that position with absolute certainty, and even Cranfield would hardly maintain that this particular incident necessarily happened at this early stage of the ministry—indeed, as he himself says, it is probably part of a pre-Marcan grouping on a topical basis. The fact that Mark has chosen to put this saying in chapter 2, therefore, should not be used in evidence against its reliability as a genuine word of Jesus.

Let us look a little more closely at these two sayings in chapter 2. The first and most striking thing which we notice in both these sayings is that they are concerned with the *authority* of the Son of man. Both occur in conflict stories, where the activity of either Jesus or his disciples is being questioned; in both cases Jesus replies by appealing to the authority of the Son of man. Once again we should ask: Why as Son of man? Is it because, once again, the authority belongs to the Son of man as Son of man?

In the first story Jesus claims authority to forgive sins—an

[15] *The Gospel According to Saint Mark*, p. 118.

50

authority which goes far beyond anything which other men possess, for, as the scribes rightly comment, only God can forgive sins. When Jesus claims the authority to forgive sins, he is claiming that he has been invested with the authority of God himself, that he is acting as God's representative and with his power. There is no indication in Jewish thought that even the Messiah was ever credited with the authority to forgive sins. Nor, of course, was the Son of man. But it is significant that the Son of man is given kingdom and rule by God and acts as God's representative—on the earth; he acts as judge. If anyone on earth is given the authority to forgive sins, then one would expect it to be the Son of man.

The second saying is concerned with the authority of the Son of man over the sabbath. The sabbath was made for man, we are told—which takes us back to the purpose of creation —and the Son of man is lord of the sabbath. It is perhaps relevant to point out that according to Jewish belief the sabbath was not given to all men to enjoy, but to Israel alone.[16] One is not surprised, then, to find that the Son of man, who in Daniel represents the saints of Israel, is Lord of the sabbath.

Now it seems to me extremely significant that both these sayings, whose authenticity is so often denied, are concerned, like all the other "Son of man" sayings, with authority. This fact suggests that they, too, represent an integral part of the "Son of man" concept. It may be objected that the idea of Jesus exercising authority now as Son of man is incompatible with the Danielic picture, where vindication and glory lie in the future. But this is to overlook the fact which we have already noticed, that in Daniel the Son of man already exists (in the saints of Israel) and that by right authority already belongs to him. It is because the Son of man's claim to authority is re-

[16] Jubilees 2:17-31.

51

jected, that he suffers and dies. It is, then, significant that Mark has placed these two incidents where he has—and where everyone thinks he ought not to have put them—namely at the beginning of his gospel, in disputes between Jesus and his opponents. For if we accept Mark's picture, then we find that he has set clearly before us in logical sequence the three aspects of the authority of the Son of man: Jesus claims authority as Son of man—a claim which is not understood by the people, and which is rejected by the scribes and Pharisees; their rejection of his authority leads to a plot to destroy him, but his claim will be vindicated—the Son of man will be seen in glory. Authority claimed, rejected, vindicated—in Mark the three groups of "Son of man" sayings belong together.

I would not be so rash as to suggest that all these sayings are "authentic." I merely wish to suggest that there is a coherence and reasonableness in the three groups: that perhaps together they may lead us back to the truth about the term "Son of man," used to symbolize the authority given to Jesus.

# V

If this interpretation of the Son of man is correct, then I suggest that the self-identification of Jesus with the Son of man is *not* psychologically incredible, and that the various strands of tradition in the Gospels do form a coherent whole. If this is so, then the onus of proof is on those who *deny* the traditional view that Jesus spoke of himself as Son of man, for the evidence of the Gospel sayings is against them. In this case the term is of supreme importance for our understanding of Jesus' own interpretation of his person and work. Moreover, we find that it is not simply a convenient self-designation, but a term which sums up the nature and authority of Jesus and the claims which he makes upon men, which are rooted in his own relationship of obedience to God.

As Son of man, Jesus stands as the fulfillment of the Old Testament hope for Israel which had never been fulfilled. But more: for in him the purpose of creation is fulfilled. In Jesus we see man as he was intended to be, as he was created by God, fully obedient to God's will, and therefore entrusted with authority and dominion over the world. The finality of Christ is seen in the fulfillment of God's purposes for man and for the world. The results are not confined to one man, however; those who join themselves to Jesus may expect to share in his experience; those who follow him will tread in the same path of obedience, suffering, and vindication, not in their own strength, but because they are disciples of Jesus; it is their attitude to him which is all important. The disciple cannot escape the path of suffering, for the scandal of the gospel is a crucified Messiah. No doubt it is paradoxical to speak of the finality of Christ in terms of a suffering Son of man. But when authority is denied, suffering is inevitable, and those who accept the authority of the Son of man must expect to share his suffering. Yet the Christian looks beyond, to the vindication of the Son of man and his followers, when the authority of the Son of man is finally acknowledged. The term "Son of man" contains in a nutshell the answer to the problem of the world's rejection of the Christian claim for the finality of Christ.

I suggested at the beginning of this chapter that the ideas conveyed in the term "Son of man" perhaps underlie much of the rest of the New Testament's Christology. Let me finish by mentioning the most important parallel, which is seen in the Pauline doctrine of the finality of Christ in terms of the Second Adam. For Paul, Adam is the type of the greater one who follows him, Christ, whose obedience to God's command reverses the disastrous results of Adam's fall [17]; it is because of his obedience to God's command that Christ is vindicated and exalted and given the name of "Lord." [18] But not only Christ; those who are joined to him—those who are in Christ—share with him suffering, death, resurrection, and exaltation. It is in Christ that man is restored and renewed in the image of his creator.[19] And not only man. For the final result of Christ's obedience is to be worked out in terms of the entire universe, which was subjected to futility as a consequence of Adam's sin[20]; with the final revelation of the glory of those who are, in Christ, sons of God, the creation itself will be released from the bondage of corruption which now shackles it and be renewed according to God's purpose. It is here, perhaps, that we have the germ of the idea of the cosmic Christ developed in Colossians, where Christ, ruler of the world and triumphant over the usurping powers, stands within the created order and yet over against it, at once firstborn among many brethren and agent of the cosmic salvation. It is Christ, the perfect image of the invisible God, in whom and through whom and for whom all things were created, and in whom all things hold together.

[17] Rom. 5:12-21.
[18] Phil. 2:5-11.
[19] Col. 3:10; II Cor. 3:18.
[20] Rom. 8:18-22.

# 3

## WORD, WISDOM, AND PROCESS

As a Christian I believe that Jesus Christ is of universal and decisive significance. I am committed to the belief that Jesus is Lord. As a Christian professionally and personally concerned with trends in current thought and present apologetic possibilities, I am convinced that we need a new appreciation of these truths about the Lordship of Christ affirmed traditionally in terms of word and wisdom. We need, and have the opportunity for, a new understanding of the cosmic significance of Jesus which will match our modern understanding of the cosmos. Unless this understanding of Jesus and the modern understanding of the cosmos are brought together, we shall be failing in preaching the gospel for our age. We shall also be leaving humanity to be swamped in the apparent vastness and indifference of that cosmos as we are now coming to understand it. But when I consider making some attempt to contribute to this task, I find myself faced with an extremely daunting initial question. What are the grounds for holding that speaking of Jesus in terms of word and wisdom is anything more than outmoded mythology, philosophy, and cosmology?

I do not find myself able to agree that it is good enough for me that Paul used such language, still less that the early church developed such language. Nor do I find it sufficient when, say, some Whiteheadian enthusiastically undertakes to show me

55

that a metaphysical view of the cosmic process allegedly (and probably largely actually) rooted in modern scientific developments positively underwrites, or is completed by cosmic assertions about, Jesus Christ. Still less am I easily cheered by Tillichian assertions that the new being in Jesus assures me that ultimate reality is both ultimate and real. The Pauline language is too much wrought out of an ancient world view for me to have any immediate conviction that it still says anything. Metaphysical language troubles me because, however neatly it coheres in itself and however plausibly it seems to correspond to generally accepted facts about the world, I always suspect that several other coherent systems using metaphysical language could be constructed. Correspondence to facts in such systems is achieved only by selection of facts and by definition of correspondence. Metaphysical systems as clues to the meaning of the universe seems to get one no further than the comment "Well, maybe," uttered in tones varying from wistful respect to skeptical scorn. This ties up with the basic worry as to whether it is proper to use terms such as "Ultimate Reality" with capital letters at all. Capital letters suggest importance and value. But the fundamental question is precisely whether the cosmic stuff of the universe is in any way interested in or capable of being related to importance and value. The possibility of making cosmic assertions of any sort on any basis seems exceedingly thin. It seems more than ever necessary, therefore, to look at cosmic assertions about Jesus as near their origin as we can get and to ask not only, "What did Paul mean?" but also, "Why did he feel himself justified in meaning this?" before we can go on and ask whether and in what way we may meaningfully use similar assertions. What follows is the merest sketch of the method and approach which the situation seems to me to require.

In Colossians Paul is addressing himself to a particular situation on the basis of a particular position which he has already reached. From that position in addressing the situation he reaches the "cosmic affirmations" which he makes about Jesus. Now I said above that the Pauline language is too much wrought out of an ancient world view for it to be *immediately* accepted as meaningful. This does not imply that it cannot be eventually accepted as meaningful; we have first to see if we can map out what I might be allowed to call the logic of the mythology.

The terms in which he makes his assertions may well come from an interplay of terms used in early Gnostic-like speculations about the universe and Jewish wisdom speculation, which is itself a mixture of Old Testament talk about the Word, language about Isis and her like, and smatterings of Hellenistic philosophy. These sources of the terminology lie in language which can properly be called mythological. For the language is used to tell stories about the universe and the human predicament, which stories draw on other stories. The language gets its force primarily from the part it plays in the stories. (For example, much of the language used in Proverbs 8 and Wisdom 7 is living and available for living use because it is language about a goddess who has an existence and power through her temples, her cult, her mythical "history," and so on.) The language does not depend for its initial force on the fact that it is a scientifically accurate description either of what did historically happen or of the way things actually are. It gets its force from the stories, and so it is mythological.

Further, one can often trace the etiology of these myths. The way in which one myth influences another can be perceived, as can the combination which a particular person makes of particular myths under the influence of his own particular philosophy so as to produce new uses of the language in the older stories. W. L. Knox does a great deal of this with varying degrees of plausibility and illumination in his *St. Paul and the Church of the Gentiles*. But the etiology of the details of the mythological language which a man uses still does not necessarily either explain or settle what he uses this language for. The source of the language in which a man expresses himself is not necessarily the decisive clue either to what he means by the language or to the reasons which he has for meaning what he does mean. Mythological language can be as reasonably used to say reasonable things as any other language—all of which has to have some degree of symbolism and all of which takes its force from the patterns in which it is customarily used. Thus to attempt to discern the logic of the use of mythological language is to attempt to see the structure of the language's use and to see whether that structure has a reasonable basis and is used to make a reasonable and comprehensive point.

Our problem, then, is whether the language and speaking of Jesus directly or by implication as the Word and Wisdom of God has a discernible structure in its use; whether it has a recognizable basis for its use which enables us both to recognize its meaning and to judge that the meaning can be valid for us. As a pilot experiment for this type of investigation I am concerned with the first chapter of Colossians. Here the basis from which Paul starts is the preaching of the gospel concerning Jesus, the acceptance of this among those to whom he is writing, and the effects of this acceptance among them and others like them elsewhere.

The basis for Paul's preaching of this gospel lies primarily in his own experience. This fact lies behind his description of himself as "apostle of Christ Jesus through the will of God" (1:1 ASV). But while his personal experience (whatever lies behind and in the "Damascus road" event) is clearly primary for Paul (cf. his perhaps overstressed claims for independence of the apostles in Galatians), that experience receives its interpreting context and its validation as something more than a merely subjective and private experience from its recognizable similarity with the experience and interpretation of those apostles and others who were believers in Jesus before him (cf. e.g., Gal. 1:18-20; 2:1-10; I Cor. 15:1-11). Here it is very important to notice that it is experience focused upon, and interpretation associated with, the particular and actual man Jesus, the occurrence of his death, and the conviction of certain potentially specifiable individuals in relation to particular experience of theirs that this crucified man was alive and powerfully active. Whatever language came to be used by those believers in or, we may say, experiencers of Jesus was intended by them to be grounded in and to be growing out of these experiences; also out of the experiences which followed in the living out of lives based individually and corporately on the acceptance of the initial experiences and interpretation.

Thus, in Colossians, after his opening greeting Paul gives thanks for their initial response to "the word of the truth of the gospel which [came] to you" (1:5 ASV) and refers to the fact that this bears fruit and increases both in the whole world and among them (vs. 6). The basis for what he has to say to them lies in the message about Jesus to which they have already assented and in the experienced effects of commitment to the living out of that assent both at Colossae and elsewhere. Now the basic shape of the message about Jesus is clear enough. It is that through, and in connection with, Jesus the Father has saved us from "the power of darkness and translated us into the kingdom of the Son of his love; in whom we have our redemption, the forgiveness of our sins" (1:13-14 ASV).

This puts us squarely back to the understanding of Jesus as the Messiah in a strictly Jewish context and against an Old Testament background. "The son of his love" or "his beloved son" is a clear reference to the Baptism narrative of Mark (reflected in the Transfiguration narratives) where Jesus is identified or designated as the one chosen or sent by God as the Son who is to fulfill God's purpose and promise for his people manifest in his choosing of King David—and thus as the one chosen by God to bring in the kingdom of God. The power of this kingdom is manifested by the defeat of the power of darkness (cf. the defeat of the demons in the Synoptic Gospels) and the defeat of the powers of darkness is the redemption which is manifested by and effective in the forgiveness of sins. For the kingdom of God is where God establishes himself as King. Since God is known above all as the Holy and Righteous God who deals with his people in terms of holiness and righteousness, the establishment of his kingdom is to be seen when the heart of resistance to him—that is sin, unholiness, and unrighteousness—is done away with. Thus the basis of the preaching of the word of the gospel is the identification of Jesus as the Messiah. The *basis* for this identification of Jesus as the Messiah lies in the disciples' experience of the livingness of Jesus after his crucifixion. The *meaning* of this Messiahship which is identified as belonging to Jesus is drawn from the whole buildup of the Jewish experience of God leading to the expectation that he would establish his kingdom in accordance with his experienced character.

But the precise way in which this Messiahship is to be understood is defined by this discovery that *Jesus* is the Messiah. Jesus could not have been recognized as the Messiah unless Messiahship already connoted something, something pointed to by the expectation of the Jews arising out of their previous experience of God and consequent hopes of God. But when Jesus was recognized to be the Messiah, as he was an actual person with an actual particular history including death in the service of the kingdom of God and vindication by living on the other side of death, his history and character now served to define that recognized Messiahship. So we are led back from the hearing of the word of the truth of the gospel which is the basis in Colossians for the further elucidation of the significance of Jesus, to the basis of this word of the gospel in the history and character of Jesus. Firstly, this is understood against the background of the Jewish experience and expectation of God. Then it is interpreted in the disciples' experience that God had vindicated and interpreted this life of the crucified Jesus by bringing him alive for them and in them. The meaning of the language about Jesus is rooted firmly in the Jews' understanding of God which arises out of all that experience which produced the Old Testament. For the fact that this meaning is rooted in truth, in the way things actually are, and is not a mere story told by men about their predicament in the world we are dependent on three things. Firstly, the evidence of the actuality of the life of Jesus; then on the reliability of the disciples' testimony to the evidence for their convictions and of the evidence of their conviction; and, finally, on the fact that this word of the gospel when assented to and followed out in individual and corporate commitment does bear fruit and increase in the particular places known to us and throughout the world.

I suggest, then, that we have located the basis of Paul's language about Jesus in Colossians in the basis of the preaching of the gospel and that this basis lies in the actual life and death of Jesus understood against the Jewish expectations of God emerging from the experience of their history—with the defining dimension of this understanding provided by the discovery of the disciples that the crucified servant of the kingdom of God was in fact powerfully alive. If the disciples' discovery that Jesus was alive as a continuing power and presence central to their relationship with God was not a real discovery of an objective fact but only an attitude of theirs,

61

an interpretation which they put upon the facts, then we have no grounds for the further language about Jesus. In other words, the question of the objectivity and reality of the resurrection of Jesus is central to the whole logic of talking about Jesus. This is what the New Testament itself would lead us to expect. The believers who made the New Testament, or whose attitude is reflected in the New Testament, did not believe that they were simply telling a story about the world, man, and God with Jesus as a character in that story. The story they felt able to tell depended on the objective reality of the Resurrection. The logical position of the New Testament is that there would be no story to tell if it were not for the Resurrection. It does violence to the whole logic of the New Testament use of mythology to give an account of the Christian faith which seeks to represent the Resurrection as simply part and, indeed, a symbolic and mythological part of the Christian story, i.e., of the attitude which Christians adopt to the world and of the story which they tell to represent that attitude. It may be the case that the Resurrection is and can only be myth and symbol. But in that case Christianity is untrue. I am well aware that many people who profess and call themselves Christians (and whose claim as individuals to be such I would not wish to deny) would deny this. I am, however, clear that this denial of theirs is partly the result of a muddled view of the admittedly uncomfortable force of the New Testament approach and partly the result of a desire to rescue Christianity from the possibility of falsification by removing it from saying anything about the world and confining it to an attitude to the world. I fear that Christianity is much more risky than that. It does say things about the world and therefore exposes itself to the judgment that what it says is either false or nonsense.

The relevance of all this to our particular inquiry is that, if talk about the Resurrection is only symbolism and mythology, then any cosmic language about Christ is a *fortiori* mythology and nothing more. I, however, am going to proceed from the assumption, because I believe it to be true, that the Resurrection is part of the *basis* of talk about Jesus and not simply talk about Jesus. I accept the testimony of the apostles that they discovered that Jesus was alive, and I do not treat this testimony as evidence simply that the apostles talked and acted as if Jesus were alive or even that Jesus' being alive consisted in the fact that the apostles so talked and acted. There is an independent fact, namely the "liveliness" of Jesus.

We return, therefore, to the assertion that the defining dimension of the understanding of Jesus which is the basis of the word of the truth of the gospel is the discovery of the disciples that the crucified servant of the kingdom of God was in fact powerfully alive. I believe that the key to the understanding of both the structure of, and the justification for, Pauline cosmic language about Jesus lies in this concept of the kingdom of God and that this can be seen as far as the language in Colossians goes from the key verses (1:13, 14 ASV—already referred to—"[God] delivered us out of the power of darkness and translated us into the kingdom of the Son of his love; in whom we have our redemption, the forgiveness of our sins"). Jesus, when his life and death are understood in the light of his resurrection, on the basis of the experience of the powerful presence of his Spirit among believers and against the background of the understanding and expectation of God as built up through the history behind and subsequent to the Old Testament, is known to be the effective focal point of the kingdom of God. Now God is already known to be the God of the whole earth, the God who "fills heaven and earth" (Jer. 23:24; cf. Isa. 6:3, etc.) Hence the scope of his kingdom is universal, hence the significance of him who is the focal point of the kingdom, "the Son of his love," is likewise universal.

63

In Colossae Paul is up against some persons (the precise nature of whose beliefs we do not need to inquire into) who claim that another understanding of the world and man's predicament and another story about the world is the really true one which "bears fruit and increases" and that it is the knowledge of this story (cf. epignōsis, epiginōskō 1:6, 9-11, etc.) which is vital for the fulfillment of salvation. Against this Paul uses deliberately Gnostic language but remains right in the center of the Old Testament understanding of the character of God and his dealings with men and asserts that the true fulfillment in knowledge is fulfillment in respect of the knowledge of the will of God and to bear fruit is to bear fruit in good works (cf. 1:9-10). We have to do with the fulfillment of the purpose of God who is concerned with persons and their moral fulfillment as persons (redemption—which is transference into the kingdom of God—is forgiveness of sins). Then he goes on to use the image and wisdom language of Jesus which makes cosmic assertions about him. This simply follows from the discovery, the basis of which I have already referred to, that Jesus is the Christ, the focal point of the kingdom of God, and the need to apply the implications of this discovery to a situation where another claim is being made about the proper understanding of, and reaction to, the human situation in the universe as we experience it.

Since Jesus is of universal significance because he is the Christ of the God of the whole earth, it must always be the case that any claim about the true way of life required by a true understanding of the world and man's place in it has to be confronted with this universal significance of Jesus and the content of this significance which is given by the life and history of Jesus, understood against the background of its Old Testament context and in the light of the Resurrection. Conversely, any illumination which men may validly obtain from their

own observations of, and reflections upon, their situation in the
universe which can be seen to be consistent with the purpose
and pattern of God's character and action as that is seen
focused in Jesus can be properly used to extend an understanding of the significance of him who is the Christ of the God
who is known as the God of this whole universe.

And there is a third point which refers directly to our concern about the logic of mythology. Any set of images which
have been used to tell a cosmic story in some mythology or
other can be validly used as part of the fruitful assertion of this
universal significance of Jesus and as part of the faithful exploration of the further implications of this universal significance of Jesus. In such a use, however, great care has to be taken
to ensure that the use of the mythology is controlled by the
basic faithful understanding of Jesus which is determined by
his place in relation to the Old Testament background, the
shape of the actualities of his life and death, and the fact of his
resurrection. It is exceedingly difficult at any given stage of the
exploration of the significance of Jesus to determine which of
two situations obtains. The first is when the current powerful
and evocative mythology is being used as the servant of the
further understanding of the significance of Jesus and of the
consequent significance of our life in the world as we have now
come to understand it. The second is when the mythology is
dominating the understanding of Jesus and of our place in the
world so that Jesus has become simply part of the story which
we feel obliged to tell about the world, and Jesus takes his
"color" from that story rather than giving his color to it. The
first position is Christian, the second is Gnostic, and I see no
reason to suppose either from history or from logic that we
shall ever be free from the difficulties of distinguishing one
from the other until the Last Day.

I would venture to suggest, however, at this present day, that Bultmann's refusal to give any weight to *historie* and to rely on *geschichte* is a modern version of just that refusal to face the risk of the involvement of the reality of God in the concrete reality of the world which is unquestionably Gnostic. (I would also maintain that Bultmann's concerns are unquestionably Christian and that his questions and investigations must be faced and dealt with, not ignored and written off, if we are to speak powerfully of the Christian faith in the modern situation). The risk of historicity is the risk of being so much a part of an actual historical situation that there is a repeated risk of seeming in every fresh historical situation to be simply part of some outmoded and now nonsensical mythology. But this risk is of the essence of "the word of the truth of the gospel." Without the basis of this historicity, taken as such on the testimony of the first apostles, in themselves and as part of the first Christian community, and of the basis of the fruit which assent to this testimony bears in committed lives "increasing in every place" we have no basis for telling any story about the world and man in the world. The approach of Paul is certainly mythological, but it is not mere mythology for it is rooted in the actualities of Jesus. It is the approach of a Bultmann or a Tillich which is, logically, mere mythology, merely a story which we choose to tell about the world although we have, ultimately, no evidence which ties it into that world but only our present consensus of opinion about "the way the world really is."

Paul, then, in Colossians is dealing with a situation in which people are telling a story about the world and man's life in it which he holds to be contrary to the understanding required by the word of the truth of the gospel as it is based in the actualities of Jesus. This story is told (of course, as the true story with consequent demands for a corresponding way of life—one ought to accept the universe and live accordingly) by men who apparently stress that the true God is invisible (cf. 1:15—eikōn tou theou tou aoratou) and that there must be a proper understanding of the true wholeness of things (the plerōma). They apparently require, therefore, that Jesus should take his proper place in an understanding which stresses the utter transcendence of the real God and a particular view of the sum total of the realities of the world. But Paul has a gospel to preach precisely because *Jesus* is the focal point of the kingdom, i.e., the place where and the person in whom the purpose of God for the establishment of that state of affairs which takes its pattern from the pattern of his character is to be seen and to be encountered. Against the use of Jesus in a pattern which is false to this he therefore restates the believed truth about Jesus by saying that it is Jesus who is the "image of the invisible God, the first-born of all creation" (Col. 1:15). This is simply to say that the pattern of the character of God, and therefore the purpose and pattern which underlies the whole of creation, is presented to us in, and in connection with, Jesus. And if Jesus is the focal point and person for the establishment of the kingdom of God in relation to the realities of this world then this is so.

Further it is perfectly proper to restate the significance of Jesus in relation to the realities of the world as a whole and to our life in that world in language taken from talk about the wisdom of God. For *that* language, however much it is language influenced by the mythology of goddesses and by particular forms of Greek philosophy, is used in the biblical and Jewish tradition to talk about the relation between the character of God, the pattern and purpose of creation, and the way in which God enables man to enter into, understand and take part in fulfilling, those patterns and purposes. Since Jesus is understood and proclaimed as the person in whom these purposes of

God are finally vindicated in the actualities of the world and since it is the experience of Paul and those with him "in Christ" that it is in, and in connection with, Jesus that the power of God to fulfill the pattern of his purposes is actually encountered in individuals and in the community life, then to talk about Jesus in wisdom language is a perfectly logical thing to do.

To fully evaluate and validate wisdom language about Jesus it would be necessary to investigate all the relevant language in Colossians and in such passages as II Cor. 4:1-6 and I Cor. 1 and 2 on these lines together with a further examination of such passages as Proverbs 8 and Wisdom 7. A similar investigation can be made of the language which talks about Jesus in terms of "Word." Here, I believe, the basic structure of the language would turn out to be not so much that of talk about the relation between the character of God and the pattern of the universe but of talk about the effective and powerful communication of God's will for, firstly, his "peculiar" people and then for men at large in the universe. Here again, the centrality of Jesus understood primarily on the basis of the recognition of his centrality to the kingdom of God would justify the application of this language to him as long as the language was used in a manner appropriate to the actualities of Jesus' life. The most famous and seminal example of this control of the language by the life of Jesus as that language is used to speak of Jesus is, of course, John 1:14—"the Word became flesh." But I fear I have no time in this present chapter to work out my own program further.

What I have been seeking to do is to begin to prepare a case for the argument that language drawn from mythology, from current stories about the nature of the world and of man's condition and possibilities in the world, can be both comprehensibly and validly used to express the significance of Jesus, providing the language can be seen to be related to the actualities of the life of Jesus and the defining understanding of the significance of Jesus which arose for the first apostles and disciples. Under such circumstances we do have a valid basis for language such as wisdom language and word language which is making assertions about the significance of Jesus in the form of assertions about the underlying pattern and purpose of the universe and about the way in which men individually and corporately can be related to that pattern. This is a perfectly valid way of talking for Christians, and it is, moreover, a way in which Christians are making assertions about the way things really are and not just talking about their subjective attitude to the universe.

The full working out of *this* program with regard to the biblical use of this language would be a preparation for two further stages in the program. The first would be to investigate the developments in the cosmic language about Jesus Christ which went on from the second century onward and is to be notably encountered in such works as the *De Incarnatione* of St. Athanasius and is reflected in the classical creeds and dogmatic statements. The purpose of this investigation would be to see how far this development is still a justifiable restatement of the centrality of Jesus related to the basis of the gospel in the actuality of Jesus, to the fruit of the gospel in the lives of the believers, and to the current understanding of the realities of the universe then prevailing.

When this part of the program is worked through, we should then be in a position to consider how Christians today are called upon to make assertions about our understanding of the realities of the universe and of man's place in that universe, once again in the light of the centrality of Jesus which is at the basis of the gospel, combined with the fruits of commitment to that gospel *and* our current understanding of the realities of the universe. It is here, I believe, we shall find that word and wisdom language needs to be related to process language for I believe that our present understanding of patterns large and small in the universe is very largely a process one. What this restatement should enable us to do is to show that the basic gospel centered on Jesus Christ gives us grounds for claiming that the process and processes of the universe are to be understood in relation to the word and wisdom of the God and Father of Jesus so that we may face these processes and be part of these processes with every hope not of disappearance into cosmic randomness but of personal fulfillment and of the fulfillment of personality.

# 4

## NON-CHRISTIAN VIEWS OF CHRIST

### Buddhism

There appears to be a growing tendency among the Western people to take an interest in the teachings of other races and not infrequently to seek a better understanding of their own Christian religious teachings in relation to other religions. Among such non-Christian religions, Buddhism is receiving great attention.

It is interesting to note that certain eminent Christian religious dignitaries are making an effort to bring about a synthesis between Buddhist and Christian teachings. Whatever be the motive in their attempts, one significant point may be stressed. If the intention of such Western writers is to bring about religious harmony among nations aiming at tolerance, peace, and the progress of mankind, this indeed deserves the highest credit. Unfortunately, however, many of the observations made by people of the caliber of the Reverend George Appleton are very misleading. It is very regrettable that many non-Buddhist Western writers are misrepresenting the facts regarding the Buddhist system of thought.

Not only the non-Buddhist writers but some of the well-known Western writers who have adopted the Buddhist religion also misrepresent these teachings, because they do not fully understand them. I am very grateful, therefore, for the opportunity of presenting the Buddhist point of view to the best of my ability in the short space at my disposal.

Siddhartha Gautama, the founder of the Buddhist system of thought, was born in India as a man in the the sixth century B.C. and lived as a man and passed away as a man. He was a man, no doubt, but he was an extraordinary man (Acchariya manusso). At no time did the founder of this system of thought expect his followers to regard him as a divine being. He never asked his disciples to believe anything he said without appealing to their reason. His attitude to knowledge was absolutely liberal. Freedom of thought, freedom of speech, respect for other people's views, and tolerance of other systems of thought, were his most outstanding features.

As examples of his liberality of thought, he cut right across the contemporary caste system, which denied religious instruction to any but members of the privileged classes, and then only to the males, by making his teaching available to people of all classes, castes, and races, and to both the sexes, and he sought to correct the indifference of his countrymen to the sufferings of animals by strongly denouncing animal sacrifice.

## MAN'S KNOWLEDGE OF GOD

It is recorded that when a group named the Kalamas asked his advice on how they could come to understand truth, Buddha laid down the general principle leading to knowledge, as follows: "Do not believe a thing just because it has been handed down to you for generations; do not believe a thing just because it has been laid down in the scriptures; do not believe a thing just because it is said by a person whom you respect; but when you yourself find that it is reasonable and rational, then accept; otherwise reject."

This, I believe, is the first charter of free inquiry ever given to man. The Buddha has given due place to man's intelligence and to his ability to comprehend truth. Nothing said in the Buddhist texts occupies the place of commandments or of oracles. The general policy which Buddha advocated throughout his mission of forty-five years was: "Come and see for yourselves" (*Ehi Passiko*).

Dogmatic acceptance of what he said is never found in his system of thought. The right to disagree was always present in his teachings. The pupil might disagree, and he had freedom to ask counter-questions of the teacher. So his disciples could ask questions of the Buddha and disagree with him.

The entire system of Buddhist thought arose as a result of Buddha's personal experience in human society. As a prince, in his early stage of life he grew up with all manner of comforts and luxuries. Recognizing the transitory nature of all things, he gradually came to realize the nature of things as they are. This realization was accomplished while being a human being associating himself with his fellow beings. The attainment of omniscience, the highest possible state of perfection which a living being can reach, was accomplished by Buddha through his own personal experience.

The enlightenment which he obtained was not revealed to him by any supernatural being. The beautiful and natural utterances made by Buddha immediately after his attainment of enlightenment are worthy of mention:

| | |
|---|---|
| *Cakkhum udapadi* | Eye arose |
| *Panna udapādi* | Wisdom arose |
| *Vijjā udapādi* | Knowledge arose |
| *Aloko udapādi* | Light arose |

This description given on the attainment of enlightenment by the Buddha is quite human and natural indeed. His effort was concentrated on finding the root causes of man's existence, his continuity, and his release. In this connection the scientific explanation which is known as the "Theory of Causal Relation" (*Paticca samuppada*) was expounded.

Teaching on the origin of the world was not one of Buddha's functions. He took it for granted that something called the world appeared to exist which is not permanent. He saw the character of change as inherent in it. Hence he never bothered to make a detailed analysis of the world as a whole. His concern was focused on man and his destiny. He dismissed all metaphysical speculation as valueless and reproved any of his disciples indulging in it.

His was the world of a teacher—the World Teacher (*Loka Guru*). He may be well compared to a physician who prescribed medicine for sickness. The Buddha considered people in general as sick. Hence prescribing a suitable prescription was considered an urgent matter. Thus the message of Buddha was expounded.

### THE WAY TO SALVATION

The Buddha was fully aware of the belief in revelation commonly found in the Hindu society of India. But he was not content with such "revealed doctrines" and expounded a middle path through which salvation could be achieved. The concept of God or *Brahman* was not unknown to him. Not being satisfied with popular interpretations of theistic concepts he made the following observations on this belief: "The traditional observances of taking refuge in higher and lower gods by man were attributed to fear."

Not knowing the cause of wind, fire, rain, disease, and other disturbing phenomena, people in primitive societies attributed these to some kind of supernatural powers generally attributed to gods. Both monotheism and polytheism are found in ancient

Indian society and their influence is still being spread here and there.

"Fear" is mentioned in Buddhism. But it is not directed to any external being, natural or supernatural. Fear for committing evil deeds, speech, and thoughts is encouraged because committing such actions will bring back adverse results upon the person who commits those acts. It is the effect of the actions that brings back results, no agent is instrumental in this. It is said there is no doer for action, so there exists no person who receives the results of the actions. It is only the phenomenon that acts.

It is said that an individual is constantly being burnt by elevenfold fires. At times individuals are burnt by lust, on other occasions they are burnt by anger, decay, death, grief, malice, lamentation, discontent, and hatred. It is for such internal defilements an individual may be afraid of, not of any other external forces.

The concept of "Self" or "Atman" is necessarily a non-Buddhistic theory. Some Christian writers try to make us believe there does not exist a lower self or a higher self in the Buddhist system of teaching. Of course the popular terminology "Self" or "Atta" is commonly used in our day-to-day language when referring to individuals. This is an unavoidable usage because a being had to be introduced by some sign or terminology. The correct term used for the individual in Buddhist text is "Satta and Puggala," being, individual. The terms "Atta" and "Attabhāva" are found in many places. But this usage is qualified with definite principles. There are two kinds of usage in the Buddhist terminology. The one is "Sammuti Sacca" (conventional truth); the other is "Paramattha Sacca" (absolute truth). The term "Atta" or "Self" is used in the realm of conventional meaning. To Buddhists who are versed in their doctrine it has no ambiguity whatsoever.

75

At this point one might raise a question: How can a Buddhist find his salvation without having any kind of relation to God? I will try to present how a Buddhist finds his ultimate goal without references to God.

The Buddhist reduces everything in this conditioned world into three general characteristics: the universality of impermanence or change; universality of suffering or inperfection; the universality of insubstantiality or permanent ego. According to the basic Buddhist theory, there cannot exist any form of being, natural or supernatural, visible or invisible, which does not undergo change. He reflects upon the changing nature of things and does not see any values in changing things. Therefore, his endeavor is to get away from persons and things which are conditioned. The basic principle Buddhists adhere to is: If a thing is conditioned, that is impermanent. The very existence of being is conditioned. Therefore, it is not worth clinging to, and developing attachment to.

With recognition of the above, a scientific formula known as the Four Noble Truths was expounded by the Buddha. Firstly, Buddha established the theory of universal suffering or imperfection (Dukkha Sacca); secondly, the truth of the origin of suffering (Dukkha Samudaya Sacca); thirdly, truth of extinction of suffering (Dukkha Nirodha Sacca); fourthly, truth of the path that leads to the extinction of suffering (Magga Sacca).

This is the central teaching of the Buddha under which the whole system of teaching is evolved. These Four Noble Truths paved the way for the scientific explanation of becoming and extinction in man. (Causal relations—Paticca samuppada).

Not only Paticca samuppada but the Eightfold Path, which is the practical aspect of the said theories, is also expounded. This again led to the unconditioned state of mind and the final goal of Buddhism which is known as Nibbana or Nirvana.

Causal relations in the doctrine of the conditionality of all physical and mental phenomena, a doctrine which, together with that of impersonality (Anattā), forms the indispensable condition for the real understanding and realization of the Buddha's teaching, shows that the various physical and mental life-processes, conventionally called personality, man, animal, etc., are not a mere play of blind chance but the outcome of causes and conditions. Above all this doctrine (Paticca samuppāda) explains how the arising of rebirth and suffering is dependent upon conditions, and in its second part it shows how, through the removal of these conditions, all suffering must disappear. Hence Paticca samuppāda serves to elucidate the second and third Noble Truths.

Once the universality of suffering (Dukkha) is recognized, its way out has to be found. That way is the Noble Eightfold Path, the way that leads to the extinction of suffering.

1. Right understanding (Sammāditthi)
2. Right thought (Sammāsankappa)
3. Right speech (Sammavācā)
4. Right action (Sammākammanta)
5. Right livelihood (Sammāāgiva)
6. Right effort (Sammāvāyāma)
7. Right mindfulness (Sammāsati)
8. Right concentration (Sammāsamādhi)

This Eightfold Path is classified into three. First and second come under wisdom (Panna). Third, fourth, and fifth come under morality (Sila). Six, seven, and eight come under concentration (Samādhi).

77

## THE GOAL OF HISTORY

Nibbāna is a word which is misinterpreted by many writers. The more the explanations, the greater the confusion. Students of Buddhism who understand the basic theory and its gradual development will have no difficulties in understanding the term "Nibbāna." The moment one is free from all worldly fetters, he is within the realm of Nibbāna. Stopping the journey through Samsāra by way of eradicating inner defilements such as craving (Tanhā), conceit (māna), ignorance (Avijjā), and the like, one is able to attain the state of Nibbāna. It is a state of perfect freedom. The question of union with anybody does not arise. This is the bliss of emancipation.

Reference which I made earlier to the doctrine of anattā—insubstantiality—proves this point still clearer. According to the Buddhist teaching on anattā, individual existence, indeed the whole world, is nothing but a process of ever-changing phenomena which are all comprised in the five groups of existence. This process has gone on from time immemorial, before one's birth, and will go on after one's death. It will continue for endless periods of time as long, and as far, as there are conditions for it. The five groups of existence—corporeality (Rupa), feeling (Vedana), perception (Saññā), mental formations (Sankhāra) and consciousness (Viññāna), either taken separately or in combination—in no way constitute a real ego-entity or subsisting personality, and equally no self, soul, or substance can be found outside this group as their "owner."

In other words, the five groups of existence are "not self," nor do they belong to a self. In view of the impermanence and conditionality of all existence, the belief in any form of self must be regarded as an illusion.

The Buddha having analyzed the nature of insubstantiality

78

in the individual advised his disciples not to depend on other persons. In the *Dhammapada* it is stated: "Self is the protector for the self. Who else could be the protector?"

This confirms the view that the Buddhists are not expected to believe even in the founder of their religion. So what talk of believing in a supernatural God?

The attempt made by certain Christian writers to prove that there exist two types of Self—lower self and true self—is a convenient fiction to extricate themselves from the dilemma into which their reasoning had led them.

The Buddhists recognize the existence of the individual and his ever-changing nature and appeal to all that is best within him to develop himself together with the society in which he lives.

What the Buddha, the *Dhamma* or doctrine which he preached, and the *Sangha*, the community of monks, can do for him is to guide him. The individual takes Buddha as a guide, *Dhamma* as a guide, and *Sangha* as a guide, but not as saviors. Actions committed by the individual either in the past or the present will determine the destiny of such individuals. This theory, known as *Kamma*, or *Karma*, is one of the major teachings of the Buddha. It is wrongly stated by certain writers that it is only past *Kamma* that matters. This is not true. Present *Kamma* has a tremendous influence on the destiny of the individual. At the same time, I can be quite certain that this theory of *Kamma* cannot in any way be identified with the Christian belief in God.

The Buddhists cannot tolerate deliberate misinterpretations being made by certain Christian dignitaries regarding Buddhist teaching. The Buddhists are entirely in favor of better understanding between religions, as well as between nations, but they do deplore intellectual dishonesty. Such attitudes will not in any way contribute toward better religious harmony.

79

## Sikhism

The Christian claim to the finality of Christ has been current since the earliest times of Christianity. So great was the historic impact of the personality of Christ among his immediate disciples and followers that they could not conceive of any other teacher of mankind who could be equally great. Naturally, the disciples had not heard of the Lord Buddha, nor of any other previous teacher apart from the Hebrew prophets, and at that time Mohammed had not arisen nor had any of the Sikh Gurus appeared. They could not be blamed, therefore, if they accorded to Jesus Christ the status of an unique, once and for all, manifestation of the Divine on earth. Moreover, the scriptures, which were written a considerable time after the death of Christ, record stories about him and sayings which reveal the personality of a mystic whose sometimes enigmatic words could have been open to various interpretations. Some other religions also claim to have found the final answer to man's spiritual destiny, and the belief that eventually all mankind must either be redeemed through one exclusive and supreme faith, or else be cast into eternal damnation, is not entirely exclusive to Christianity. The Sikh religion, however, makes no such claim, nor does it claim for its Ten Gurus, or teachers, any unique place in history or any special kind of divinity. Yet it does claim to provide for the devotees of God a path to salvation equal to that of any other religion, and much more simple to understand than that of some.

In order to understand the Sikh attitude toward Christianity, and indeed, toward all other religions, it is necessary to examine briefly the roots and origins of the Sikh religion. It owes its birth to a religious reformation which took place in India in the fifteenth century. Its founder was a teacher or Guru called Nanak who was born in 1469. Nanak came from a high-caste Hindu family; he was deeply interested in all forms of religion, and he studied Islam as well as Hinduism; he soon became well versed in the numerous religious and philosophic theories which were then current in India. Although Guru Nanak traveled widely to Ceylon, Northeast India, the outskirts of Tibet, Arabia, and Mecca, there is no record of his ever having come into contact with any form of Christianity, though Dr. A. C. Bouquet of Cambridge sees in Sikhism some similarity with Christianity. However, this similarity may easily have descended through Islam and the practical Sufism taught by Kabir immediately prior to Nanak in the Punjab.

Nanak had no quarrel with the highest principles of Hinduism and Islam, but he was highly dissatisfied with the way in which they were practiced and taught. Popular religion had largely degenerated into superstition, idol worship, intolerance, hypocrisy, and profiteering. Nanak's main concern was to teach the oneness of God; the way in which any human being could become aware of the presence of God, and the equality and brotherhood of all mankind. Thus, he first taught to his followers the Mool Mantra, a verse which appears at the beginning of the Guru Granth Sahib, the Sikh holy book:

> There is One God,
> His name is Truth,
> The All-pervading Creator;
> Without fear, without hatred;
> Immortal, unborn, self-existent.
> The Enlightener, by Grace.
> True in the beginning; True throughout the ages;
> True even now, Nanak, and forever shall be True.

When Nanak said that God is unborn, he meant this to be in contradiction to the Hindu belief in avataras, a theory that the Divine soul is manifested on earth from time to time in the form of an earthly creature, sometimes a human being. God himself is unbounded and formless, said Nanak, therefore no single living creature can contain him. God is all-pervading; he is the reality behind all creation; he is both the matter and mind of all things; he is the first cause of all causes. His will guides the universe and works within it for his own purposes. Every being is illumined by his divine spark; every soul is a part of himself. This being the belief and teaching of Guru Nanak, it would have been impossible for him to accept the idea of a special incarnation, or the Christian claim to the divinity of Christ, or the uniqueness of his appearance in the course of history. Nanak would say instead, that God's light is manifest in all human beings, that man himself has sprung from the Divine, and that at the end of his journey of life, he is destined eventually to reach God again and merge his spark in the Light of all Lights. Thus, all men are equally the children of God, and no one can claim to be God's son more than another. The verse known as the Arti, by Guru Nanak, expresses the all-pervading nature of God:

The firmament is Your salver, Your lamps the sun and moon;
The galaxies of stars are like scattered pearls.
Your incense is the scent of sandalwood, Your fan the breeze;
The forests are Your flowers, O Lord of Light.
What divine worship is this!
O Destroyer of birth, this worship is Yours.
The unstruck notes of heaven are Your drums.
You have a thousand eyes and yet no eye;
A thousand forms are Yours, yet not one form.
You have a thousand stainless feet, and yet no foot;
A thousand nostrils Yours, yet not one nose.

All this is Your fascinating play.
The light which dwells in all is Your light, Lord.
By the Guru's word revealed, it illumines everything.
This worship is the true one, it is Your delight, O God.
O Lord, my mind longs for Your lotus feet, as the honey-bee longs
    for the flowers:
Night and day I thirst for them.
Give the water of Your favour to the sarang, Nanak,
That he may dwell in the love of Your name.

### MAN'S KNOWLEDGE OF GOD

The Guru maintained that God can reveal himself to man through all religions. One of the fundamental precepts of the Sikh religion is tolerance and respect for all other faiths, even where there is disagreement on details of belief. Guru Nanak taught that, provided the rules of conduct of a religion are carried out with sincerity and a pure heart and are directed toward the love and service of mankind, any faith can lead the devotee to God. Without love and with only the mechanical observance of prayers, fasts, and rituals, there can be no spiritual progress. In Sikhism God is revealed to man through the Gurus' word: the divinely inspired utterances of the ten Sikh Gurus which are recorded in the Guru Granth Sahib. He is also revealed through the lives and examples of the Gurus, saints, prophets and holy men of any religion. This is known to the Sikhs as sadh sangat, the society of the saints with whom the Sikh is supposed to keep company in order to be inspired by them, to learn from them and to follow their example. This is the manifest aspect of God. But the Sikh must also remember that God exists in the unmanifested aspect so that his attributes are also described by negative terms, such as formless, colorless, unknowable, or indescribable.

83

The Finality of Christ

## THE WAY TO SALVATION

Whether man receives this revelation of God depends on his own efforts. If he opens his mind to the word of the Guru, to the good influence of the saints, if he leads a good and useful life, and remembers God's name in his heart, he may, with the aid of God's grace, achieve some inner vision of the divine. The Sikh way to God is made clear in the scriptures which were written and compiled by Guru Nanak and six of his nine successors. Briefly, the way is this: that after having gone through numerous births in lower forms of life, the soul or the spark of divinity which originally came from God, eventually takes birth in human form. Then, being human, with the additional attributes of free will, speech, and the choice of doing good or evil, the spirit has his opportunity to realize his true identity and eventually to seek reconciliation and reunion with God. By God's grace man may come into contact with a Guru or teacher who can show him the way to salvation. The Guru is not in any sense to be regarded in the same way that the Christians regard Christ. He is not in any special way divine, but he is a man who has already trodden the path toward salvation and who has himself realized the perfect truth. He is one who knows God by personal experience and whose soul is united with God; he is a living liberated soul. The Gurus of the Sikhs were regarded in this light; they were not worshiped, but both during their lives and after they have always been deeply revered by their followers. The writings which they left are regarded as having been divinely inspired, and the holy book, the Guru Granth Sahib, is now regarded as the only Guru of the Sikhs.

Once having accepted his Guru, man must follow the Guru's teaching with the utmost devotion and faith. The Sikh discipline teaches him to remember God's name constantly, to

84

immerse his soul in the living presence of God day and night, during all his worldly activities. The Sikh must lead an active life of love and service to his fellow men and with the obligations and duties of his family and household. This was the way of life practiced and taught by the Gurus. It was not the Guru's function to act as an intercessor between God and man, nor to demonstrate God's love for mankind. In Sikh philosophy man and God need no one to intercede, and there is no necessity for any demonstration of love to be made. God's love is completely and visibly manifest in the beauty and wonders of his creation and in his countless gifts to mankind. Therefore, God needs no son; he needs no one to create for him; he needs no single, exclusive, or unique messiah. His light is revealed to man in all things, but most brightly in those souls who, having achieved salvation themselves, stand as his messengers on earth to guide mankind in the ways of truth, righteousness, and divine love. Such people have appeared throughout history, not as divine incarnations, but as human beings, as buddhas, gurus, saints, and prophets such as Moses, Jesus, and Mohammed. The ordinary man is like a light enclosed in a glass which is dark, smoky, and opaque, so that the light within is dimmed or completely obliterated; but the saint is like a lamp with bright, clear crystal glass through which the light shines forth fully revealed in all its beauty and glory. Man's eventual salvation rests partly on his own efforts and partly on God's grace. The Guru is there to guide him; like the leader in a difficult rock climb, he finds the route, makes and tests the footholds, and stands firm with the safety rope if his disciple should slip; but the disciple himself must make the effort to climb.

Guru Nanak emphatically maintained that no amount of religiosity would help a man to salvation if he did not at the same time, lead a morally good life. He said, "There is nothing greater than Truth, but greater still is true living." The way to salvation in Sikhism is twofold: through repetition of the name or devotion, and through the service of mankind. Thus, in remembering the name, the Sikh may use any name which indicates a good and noble attribute of God. Such remembrance will elevate his soul and bring with it an increase of such attributes in himself; his actions will accordingly become nobler and purer and his life will acquire a divine purpose and sanctity. Guru Gobind Singh, the Tenth Guru who died in 1708, composed a long poem called the Jap Sahib which gives hundreds of names and attributes of God:

> I salute the Sage of Sages,
> Lord of the Worldly;
> Kindest of All,
> Sustainer of All.

However, the favorite name often uttered by Sikhs is "Waheguru," Wonderful Lord.

Service is essential for the good of man's soul and for the betterment of all mankind. It is true to say that no man can be completely happy while any of his brethren still suffer. If God is seen to be in all mankind, then to serve mankind is also to serve God, while to reject the cry of humanity is to turn one's back on God. This, at least, is one point on which Christians and Sikhs would agree. On the other hand, if man disregards God and the love and service of mankind; if he leads a life of sin, hatred, and selfishness, he will be bound to suffer eventually for his acts. He will reap what he has sown, and, according to Sikh belief, he will continue to be reborn on this earth and to suffer the consequences of his evildoing until he turns toward God and tries to do good. Some Sikhs, like some Christians, believe in heavens and hells as actual places to which the spirit is assigned, but there is at least no doubt that they do exist as states of mind and that people suffer in them accordingly; but for the Sikh, there is no permanent hell and there is no final and irrevocable condemnation even for the worst of evildoers, for all may have an endless number of opportunities to escape from the rounds of rebirth and reach perfect Truth.

## THE GOAL OF HISTORY

There are many apparent differences between religions, but it is my belief that such contradictions as there are, are more frequently due to differences in individual interpretation and diverging viewpoints of the same center of reality. According to Christianity, as I understand it, the final end of history would be the establishment of Christ's rule over all mankind. Here also, much depends on interpretation, and this idea can be given a parallel in the Sikh belief that all souls will eventually be reunited with God. However, in Sikh cosmology, the destiny of this earth and its inhabitants is not separate or different from the destiny of the whole universe. To the Gurus God is not only the Lord and Creator of this earth nor only of the solar system. He is the ruler and source of all worlds, both spiritual and material. His domain is over the universe, the galaxy, and the millions of galaxies beyond. There is no beginning nor end of God's creation known to man, either in time or space. However, if we accept the theory of evolution (which is quite compatible with the Sikh scriptures), we can trace the beginnings of man from the first flicker of life on this earth. We can trace his progress physically and mentally, but we can only guess at the spiritual state of man in the first stages of his emerging intellect. We can guess that he must have been in a state of innocence, not being aware of good and evil and knowing no moral standards; therefore, in the beginning, he must have been incapable of doing wrong. As man's self-awareness and ego developed, so did his potentiality for doing good or evil; his fear of retribution and his capacity for mental unhappiness. At the same time—we have no idea how early in man's development—he came to be aware of the existence of God nor do we know whether early man worshiped one God, the Creator, or many nature gods or ancestor spirits. Both theories have been put forward by rival schools of thought. Dr. Martin Lings supports the theory that when man was first created, he lived in a golden age when he believed in monotheism, and that only later when he developed agriculture, and settled permanently, did he degenerate into polytheism. According to Sikhism, however, man has come, it is true, from a state of spiritual purity and innocence, but this was an innocence without knowledge; it was an untested and untried purity. Man, unaware of himself and his divine origin, was really in ignorance and without real virtue. It is only when he has passed through the fire of life and when he has been tried to the utmost that his strength and virtue are proven and his final perfection becomes unassailable.

As early man did not know the real nature of God, he invented a kind of God who, like himself, was motivated by desire, anger, self-interest, love, and hatred. Such were the many gods of the ancients, and even the unique god of the early Hebrews was attributed with very human emotions. But the Hebrew concept of God gradually developed and changed as he revealed himself through Abraham, Moses, and the subsequent prophets. Unlike the other gods, he was one who demanded righteousness, holiness, and exclusive loyalty from his worshipers. This concept eventually culminated in the teaching of Jesus whose God was the divine Father of all mankind, infinitely merciful and forgiving, loving and perfect. This God wanted man to become like him in these respects: "Forgive your brother as your Father in heaven forgives you," said Jesus. Such a concept of God was certainly the highest that had ever been reached in the Western world. This idea subsequently permeated into later Jewish thought and brought about the flowering of modern Judaism. It deeply influenced Islam, founded by Mohammed who was born in A.D. 570. Mohammed preached strict monotheism and the idea of Allah, the Compassionate, the Merciful, which he developed from his early contact with both Christians and Jews and transformed into a religion particularly suited to the nature of the Arab tribes and replacing their old idolatrous religions.

Meanwhile, in the East, the religion of compassion, Buddhism, had been founded by the Lord Buddha, while the later forms of Hinduism developed the highly spiritual and ethical philosophy of the supreme Brahman manifested through the noble person of god, Krishna of the *Gita*. Both the Semitic and the Oriental traditions are the parents of the Sikh faith. Guru Nanak was influenced by the best of both Islam and Hinduism. There is no doubt that the idea of One God, the Father of mankind, as developed in Judaism and taught by Christ, came to Guru Nanak through Islam, but the notion of the all-pervading origin of all things, Brahman, is also combined with it in Sikhism. The ideals of compassion, mercy, love, and service to mankind which are part of the Sikh faith, were developed first in both Christianity and Buddhism, whereas ideas of universal brotherhood can also be found in both traditions, though certainly more strongly in Islam. Thus, not only Christianity and Christ have a unique place in history, but all the other religions as well have contributed something special to the story of mankind.

Mankind continues now, to be as diverse as he was in the past, and, although there is a certain merging of cultures and races in the modern world, it is not likely that all mankind will ever come under the spiritual sway of one special religion. Nor would this be a desirable state of affairs. People are individuals who are extremely diverse in their rates of progress and in their stages of spiritual development: each person needs a belief which accords with his own particular spiritual state, and each different path has its own special merits. It will be discovered by the sincere seeker after truth that although the orthodox beliefs of religions appear to differ widely from each other, yet the mystic who truly perceives with the inner eye of his soul, the perfect light of reality, is no longer concerned with differences between so-called "divinity" or so-called "humanity," nor with the superiority of one teacher over another. By whatever path the mystic may have reached the light, he will be able to see, as the Guru says, "The current of truth running through all religions." This being so, there is no justification for any one religious group to claim that theirs is the only true way to salvation and that it is only by following their particular master that all mankind can be saved. Thus, I firmly believe that God is merciful and loving toward all human beings, whether or not they believe in the finality of Christ. In the words of the Fifth Guru, Arjan, who died for the Sikh faith:

> He is a forgiving God; kind to the distressed,
> Responsive to love, and merciful always.
> The Divine Herdsman places Himself at the head of His
> straying flock,
> And feeds them, one and all.
> He is the Primal Being, the Cause of all causes, the
> Creator,
> The very breath of life to those who love Him.
> Whoever worships Him is cleansed,
> And is attached to love and devotion.

We are low, ignorant and devoid of virtue,
But we have come to Thy protection, O Lord of all
resources.

## A Jew Looks at Jesus

"Who do you say that I am?" Jesus asked of his disciples
(Matt. 16:15), and this question, which led to Peter's confession
of faith, still remains a crucial question, for the Jew no less
than for the gentile, today no less than nineteen hundred years
ago. It is this question I should like to discuss here. Speaking as
a Jew, from out of what I take to be the authentic tradition of
Jewish faith, what can I say about Jesus, the man of Nazareth
whom Peter hailed as the Christ?

### I

Jesus was, first of all, a great and incomparable moral teacher.
Of that there cannot be, and indeed never has been, any doubt.
His exhortations and discourses stand unrivaled in the ethical
literature of mankind. Men of all cultures and religions have
paid tribute to the inexhaustible truth and power of his moral
teaching. The Sermon on the Mount is known wherever men
anywhere have concerned themselves with the moral life, and
nowhere has it failed to stir the imagination and raise the heart
to the self-giving love which Jesus preached. By the common
testimony of mankind, this Jewish rabbi from Nazareth nineteen
hundred years ago reached the high-water mark of moral vision
and ethical teaching.

But if that were all there was to it, there would be no ques-
tion to ask and no problem to discuss. For, as a moral teacher,
Jesus stands merely as one among many, one of the rabbis of
Judaism, entirely in the line of rabbinical tradition. Scholars,

both Jewish and non-Jewish, have shown beyond the shadow of a doubt that all his moral teachings, even the most exalted, have their sources and parallels in the contemporary religious literature of the Jews, from whom he sprang and among whom he taught. It is not enough to point to the consummate synthesis that this teacher of genius achieved in his teaching. This may be granted, but it is not simply, or even primarily, as a moral teacher that Jesus confronts us as a problem and a challenge. As a moral teacher, he is a Jewish rabbi of great power and insight, drawing upon the traditional wisdom of his people. That is a great deal, but it is not enough to answer the question we are asking. We must look further.

Jesus was, on the next level, in the line of the prophets of Israel. If the prophet is the God-possessed man standing over against the community to which he belongs, bringing to bear upon it the word of the Lord in judgment and promise, then Jesus of Nazareth was a prophet in Israel, in the succession of Amos, Isaiah, Jeremiah, and Hosea. His denunciations of the corruptions and idolatries of the age, his call to repentance, his promise of divine grace for those of a broken heart and a contrite spirit, his proclamation of the new age to come as judgment and fulfillment, follows, as it was meant to follow, the pattern of the great prophets. There is, indeed, something new because of the new situation; but this newness, this speaking out of and to the condition of the time, is precisely what characterizes the living word of prophecy. Jesus, the rabbinic teacher, is also among the prophets of Israel, with clear affinities to the great prophets of the past.

But again, if that were all there was to it, there would be no question to ask and no problem to discuss, for again, neither as prophet nor as moral teacher is Jesus anything more than one among many. It is not here that his uniqueness, if uniqueness there be, is to be discovered. Jesus' prophetic proclamations follow the prophetic word of his predecessors; his denunciations of the self-righteous "scribes and Pharisees" can be abundantly paralleled in the literature of rabbinic self-criticism; the promise he held out of divine mercy for the repentant sinner was a promise which every contemporary Jew could understand even if he could not prevail upon himself to take hold of it. No, not here can we find the answer to our question—we must look still further.

## II

The Jesus that confronts us as a problem is the Jesus whom Peter confessed the Christ and whom the Fourth Gospel represents as declaring: "I am the way . . . ; no one comes to the Father, but by me" (John 14:6). What can a Jew make of this confession and this claim?

It seems to me obvious that this claim and this confession have no meaning outside the context of the faith of Israel, as defined in the Hebrew Bible, in which Judaism and Christianity alike are grounded. The persistent attempt through the centuries to throw out the Old Testament and replace it with some other so-called "preparation for the gospel," such as Greek philosophy, Hindu mysticism, or modern science, is inevitably and inescapably, however unwittingly, an attempt to destroy the biblical substance of the Christian faith, and to convert Christianity into a pagan salvation cult. Christian faith is biblical and Hebraic, or it is nothing at all.

Viewing it from the biblical-Hebraic standpoint, and in the light of a biblically defined understanding of God's redemptive purpose, what can a Jew say of the Christian church and the Christ it proclaims? It is hard to avoid the conviction that Christianity emerges, in God's plan of redemption, to open the covenant of Israel to the "nations of the world." In biblical faith it is in and through membership in the covenanted people of God that—humanly speaking—man has his standing with God and can avail himself of God's grace for redemption. "The individual Israelite," Alan Richardson has pointed out, "approaches God in virtue of his membership in the holy people. . . . In the whole of the Bible, in the Old Testament as well as the New, there is no such thing as a private personal relation between an individual and God apart from this membership in the covenantfolk." [1] Man's relation to God is essentially responsive; it is God's call, expressed in the grace of election, that gives man the possibility—from *his side*—of entering into personal relations with God. (Modern existentialism, in its very welcome emphasis on personal confrontation, has tended to forget that such confrontation is, humanly speaking, possible only *within*, and on the basis of, the covenant.) In the biblical view people outside the covenant, properly called gentiles, cannot—apart from the uncovenanted grace of God—of themselves find their way to God or meet him in personal encounter. In our modern intellectualistic, and therefore inadequate, terminology this is equivalent to saying that only the religion of Israel brings men to God; other, pagan religions, the "religions of the world," lead men away from him.

The covenant of Israel is understood by the prophets, and perhaps much earlier, as the covenant of a redeemed and redeeming community; the purpose it defines is a universal purpose, and the people it brings into being are an instrument of God for the redemption of mankind. All are to be gathered into the covenant, and within the covenant restored to a right relation to God. It is in this context that the Jew finds it possible to understand the providential role of the church, and the church to understand the never-failing providential function

[1] "Instrument of God," *Interpretation*, III (1949), 278.

of Jewry. Through Christ God's covenant with Israel is—in the fullness of time—opened to all mankind. As the one by whom and through whom the covenant of Israel is opened to mankind, Christ appears in early Christian thinking as, quite literally, an incarnate or one-man Israel. Through union in faith with him the gentile believer, the pagan of yesterday, becomes part of Israel; he therefore comes under the covenant, and thereby becomes heir to the promise of God to Israel. "If you are Christ's," Paul says, "then you are Abraham's offspring, heirs according to the promise" (Gal. 3:29). "That the blessing of Abraham might come on the gentiles through Jesus Christ"; that is how the apostle describes this aspect of Christ's redemptive work (Gal. 3:14, KJV). He admonishes recent gentile converts:

Remember that you were at that time separated from Christ, alienated from the commonwealth of Israel, and strangers to the covenants of promise. . . . But now in Christ Jesus you who once were far off have been brought near . . . so [that] you are no longer strangers and sojourners, but you are fellow citizens with the saints and members of the household of God (Eph. 2:12-19).

Solomon Groyzel, a modern Jewish writer, has—I think quite correctly—put what he takes to be Paul's meaning in these words: "He so broadened the term 'Jew' as to include in it . . . all those who transformed their lives by being faithful Christians."

Attempting to understand what has happened in terms of the divine purpose, the Jew can see Christ as he in whom God was, and is, acting for the redemption of the peoples. Through Christ a new covenant community is created—the church, the "Body of Christ." Through Christ Israel's redemptive history becomes the redemptive history of the pagan-turned-Christian, who becomes in effect an Israelite. "Through Jesus Christ," H.

# The Finality of Christ

Richard Niebuhr points out, "Christians of all races recognize the Hebrews as their fathers. . . . All that has happened to that strange and wandering people of God becomes part of their own past." [2]

Christian faith thus brings into being and defines a new covenant; but it is new not in the sense of supplanting the old, but in the sense of extending and enlarging it, very much as we speak of the new world side-by-side with the old. For with the emergence of Christianity the election and vocation of Israel are not annulled, nor does the church supersede the people of the "old covenant." The notion that it does not only renders unintelligible the survival of Jewry these nineteen hundred years; it is itself a manifestation of that spiritual pride, the pride of supersession, that goes a long way toward corrupting the meaning and power of the gospel that is proclaimed. The election of Israel remains, and its vocation remains, though it assumes a very different form in the Christian world from that which it possessed in the pre-Christian.

It is in terms of this conception of the double covenant, that the Jew can see Jesus on the level of his uniqueness. He is indeed the way—the way by and through which the peoples of the world may enter the covenant of Israel and come to serve the God of Israel, who is the Creator of the universe and the Lord of all being. "Israel," Franz Rosenzweig, the great Jewish religious philosopher, has said, "can bring the world to God only through Christianity." [3] And this "Christianity" is, of course, the extension into history of the Jesus whom Peter hailed as the Christ.

But there is also the other side of the medal. "Christianity,"

[2] *The Meaning of Revelation* (New York: The Macmillan Company, 1946), pp. 115-16.

[3] *Franz Rosenzweig: His Life and Thought*, Nahum Glatzer, ed. (New York: Schocken Books, 1953), p. 341.

96

Rosenzweig continues, "could not long remain a force for redemption without the Jew in its midst," [4] and what that means can best be seen in the words of Paul Tillich, who speaks from the Christian commitment:

It is important that there always be Judaism. It is the corrective against the paganism that goes along with Christianity . . . The Church is always in danger of adoring the gods of space in which she is ruling . . . The church is always in danger of losing her prophetic spirit . . . Therefore the prophetic spirit included in the traditions of the Synagogue is needed so long as the gods of space are in power, and that means to the end of history.[5]

Against all idolatries, Judaism proclaims: "Hear, O Israel, the Lord is our God, the Lord alone"; and this is a word which the church as well as the world, and the church because it is so immersed in the world, never ceases to need. Judaism's witness to the living God, which it is compelled to bear by its divine calling as that is expressed in history, is a witness that cannot end until all things are brought to the end of judgment and fulfillment.

Yes, each needs the other: Judaism needs Christianity, and Christianity needs Judaism. The vocation of both can be defined in common terms: to bear witness to the living God amidst the idolatries of the world. But, since the emergence of the church, and through the emergence of the church, this vocation has, as it were, been split into two parts. The Jew fulfills his vocation by "staying with God," "giving the world no rest so long as the world has not God"—to recall Jacques Maritain's unforgettable phrase.[6] The Christian can fulfill his

---

[4] *Ibid.*

[5] Quoted in A. Roy Eckardt, *Christianity and the Children of Israel* (New York: King's Crown Press, 1948), pp. 146-47.

[6] *A Christian Looks at the Jewish Question* (New York: Longmans, Green & Company, 1939), p. 29.

vocation only by "going out" to conquer the world for God. The Jew's vocation is to "stand," the Christian's to "go out"— both in the same cause of the kingdom of God. Judaism and Christianity thus represent one faith expressed in two religions —Judaism facing inward to the Jews, and Christianity facing outward to the gentiles, who, through it, are brought to the God, and under the covenant, of Israel, and therefore cease to be gentiles in the proper sense of the term. This is the unity of Judaism and Christianity, and this is why a Jew is able to see and acknowledge Jesus in his uniqueness as the way to the Father.

I know that what I say here will not satisfy those who are Christians, although they will, I hope, recognize its truth so far as it goes. And, indeed, it should not satisfy the Christian, since to the Christian, Jesus as the Christ must necessarily mean much more than he can possibly mean to the Jew. For the Jew sees Jesus as emerging from Israel and going forth; he sees him from the rear, as it were. The Christian, on the other hand, precisely because he is a Christian, will see Christ as coming toward him, in the fulness of divine grace, to claim, to judge, and to save; he meets him as Paul met him on the road to Damascus or as Peter outside Rome, face to face in confrontation. Yet this difference of perspective should not blind us to the fact that it is the same reality we see. And indeed—here again I quote Franz Rosenzweig—the two religions relate to the same truth, being equal representations of it—equal before God.[7] With God, truth is one; but for men it is irreducibly split, since the truth as men see it is confessional and conditioned by one's community of faith. This is not a vicious relativism, nor does it assert for one moment that all religions are equally valid or equally true. On the contrary, as

[7] *Franz Rosenzweig*, p. 341.

Rosenzweig puts it, man is either a pagan or a Jew or Christian.[8] The pagan, as pagan, is outside the scope of the covenant—that is what being a pagan means—though God, in his mercy, may, of course, reach out to him. Jew and Christian, on the other hand, has each his assigned position, defined in the covenant that relates him to God. Their positions, their "standpoints," being different, their views of the one truth and the one reality will be different, although both will be views of the same truth and the same reality—just as two people standing in the same room but in different corners will see the room in different perspectives and therefore somewhat differently. Each will be loyal to the truth if he speaks out the truth as he sees it, though recognizing that his truth is never quite identical with the full truth of God. This approach does not derogate from the "finality" of either Judaism or Christianity, if that is properly understood; it merely prevents our making an idol of either; both are seen as instruments in the redemptive purpose of God, though each in a different way.

In short, each—the Jew on his part and the Christian on his —sees the truth as that is to be apprehended from his perspective, defined by his covenant and his vocation. Each must stand by his truth and confess it, recognizing that insofar as he does so in integrity and wholeness of heart, he remains faithful to the God whose truth it is. Naturally, since the two see the same reality in somewhat different ways, each may see an aspect of the truth hidden to the other, and even interpret the same truth differently. But perhaps that is part of God's purpose in placing the Jew and Christian on different sectors of the fighting front of the Kingdom, so that each may bear not only the common witness to God, but also a witness against the perils, inadequacies, and temptations of the other. The witness

[8] *Ibid.*

of Christianity against the legalistic, moralistic tendencies in Judaism is a witness for which the Jew must always be grateful. And the Christian, too, it seems to me, ought to see the value of the Jewish word in this dialogue. The Christian who tends to be impatient with the Jew for refusing to see in Jesus the fulfillment and completion of God's redemptive work might pause a moment to consider whether this Jewish "obstinacy" was not itself important as an indispensable reminder of the very incompleteness of this completion, of a redemption which may indeed have come but is nevertheless yet to come. The heart of each, Jew and Christian alike, may ache, perhaps, that the other is not in his camp, seeing things his way and fighting side-by-side with him on his sector of the front; but he ought also to recognize that though the other fights on a different sector, he is also fighting the same battle for the same God, and that it is perhaps by the providence of God that they are thus separated.

## III

This, then, is how a Jew may see Jesus and the faith and church built upon the confession of him as the Christ. I realize how difficult it is for one to communicate what he has to say on this matter. "Christ," Franz Kafka, the Jew, once exclaimed, "is an abyss filled with light; one must close one's eyes if one is not to fall into it." [9] And yet speak one must. In Jesus—not merely Jesus the moral teacher, Jesus the prophetic voice, but also the Jesus whom Christians confess the Christ—Jew and Christian find their unity . . . and their difference. In answering the question, "Who do you say that I am?" Jew and Christian stand separated yet united. The unity far transcends the separa-

[9] Gustav Janouch, *Conversations with Kafka* (New York: Frederick Praeger, 1953), p. 93.

tion, however real that may be; for the two are united in their common allegiance to the living God and in their common expectation of, and longing for, the One who is to come—for the Christian, the One who came and is to come again, for the Jew the One who is promised to Israel, but for both the same Promised One. In this one faith and hope, Jew and Christian— to recall Paul Tillich's words—stand united until the end of time in the struggle for the Lord of history against the pagan and idolatrous powers that threaten to overwhelm us on every side.

# 5

## THE FINALITY OF CHRIST IN PERENNIAL
## PERSPECTIVE

### THE INCREASING DIFFICULTY OF BELIEF IN JESUS CHRIST

Christian belief was jarred by the shock-waves of modern science in the nineteenth century. Then for a generation or two the common mind of the Christian community regained its equilibrium, only to be staggered more seriously by another wave of scientific discovery in the mid-twentieth century. We thought we had grasped some idea of the vastness of space and the complexity of our little planet. But as the scientists peer beyond the farthest galaxies to the quasars at unimaginable distance in space and time, or as they analyze and describe the structure of inanimate matter and even of the elements of living tissue, they appear to be penetrating the realms which Christian belief has held to be the impenetrable areas of divine mystery.

Now, it is a frightening thing to contemplate the greatness of the universe and the littleness of the earth. And much less significant than the earth seems man himself. This tiny but wondrous creature is like an intelligent plankton, pondering the size and meaning of the seven oceans.

From another viewpoint, however, there is an incomprehensible vastness of the human race, the thought of which overwhelms the individual man. Existing for only a wink of time in the geological calendar, this race of upright, thinking animals is claimed by Christian faith to bear a unique resemblance to the Creator of all things. Their numbers run to countless millions. Even those presently living, if they were standing side by side, would gird the earth's equator more than forty times. For a thousand centuries has run the endless process of birth and death: opening womb, closing tomb. Man after man after man. Millions dying in infancy. Yet each of them more than a mere unit of *homo sapiens*. Each a person, each with a soul, each a private universe of experience, each a custom-made work of the Creator, each a distinctive person poured into the new mold which the Maker then destroys.

The apparent incredibility of Christian faith does not end with its claims about the personal creatures of the personal God. The Christian proclamation stretches intelligibility and credulity more than this—and even more than do the theories of the astrophysicists and cosmologists. Christians assert that at a particular point of time, just thirty-three years in the human historical continuum, in a tiny tributary of that vast river of man's earthly existence, in a malodorous cowbarn in a village of small importance, the Master Mind and Maker of this whole dazzling and virtually endless universe became man.

How can this belief be substantiated? Faithful Christians travel as pilgrims to the Holy Land, hoping to find reassurance for their faith as they look upon the places where Jesus lived and worked and died. But the effect of this visit is often twofold: it makes the historic life of Jesus seem more real; but it renders more difficult an unquestioning belief in the doctrine of incarnation. The wilderness east of Jerusalem to the Jordan River, as well as the barren hills of Galilee, lie in mute defiance of the likelihood that here, once and uniquely, the eternal

103

Word of God became man. No one need doubt that there once lived and taught in this forbiddingly rugged land a prophet of extraordinary wisdom and superior humanity. The records are dependable. But the sheer magnitude of the Christian affirmation that Jesus was true God and true man, in a unique and unrepeatable sense, makes this fundamental confession seem to outsiders no less than fantastic.

Equally unacceptable to the critical and skeptical mind, of course, is the further assertion of Christians that the life, death, and resurrection of this guileless Jew have constituted the act of God whereby men and women of all generations are enabled to enjoy a genuinely human existence and eternal communion with God.

From a natural, rational viewpoint the wonder is not that multitudes have either rejected or fallen away from this faith. The wonder is that so great a number of intelligent persons accept it, live by it, and find life's meaning in it.

## UNIQUENESS AND UNIVERSALITY

The question about Jesus Christ is unique. No other issue in the extensive repertory of man's religious thought is like that of the person and perennial effect of Jesus Christ. There may be legitimate comparisons with the tenets of other religions: the range of belief in theophanies, revelations, incarnations, miracles, as well as in prophets, teachers, deliverers, and saviors. It is irresponsible and arrogant for some Christians to deny the possibility of such comparisons with the central figures of both defunct and continuing religions. But it is at the last quite fruitless to place Jesus amongst the persons and personifications, both historical and mythological, which are the founders or focal points of diverse religions. For Christian faith Jesus is simply outside the category of Moses, Gautama the Buddha, Krishna, Mohammed, Zoroaster, and the rest. We may say that in secondary matters, such as certain of his words and deeds, Jesus is comparable to others; but in primary ones, such as the identity of his person and his relation to God and man, he is incomparable. This does not mean that as human he is comparable but as divine incomparable; but in the unity of his person as both divine and human he is incomparable.

Not only is Jesus Christ regarded and confessed as unique. He is also universal: the one who is for all. This assertion does not necessarily simplify a simple universalism with respect to the doctrine of salvation. This issue is still disputed, as in past centuries, on the ground of differing views of God's grace in electing people and of the consequences of a person's faith. Whether one be persuaded of a narrow or a very wide expectation of salvation, however, as a Christian he cannot reject the universality of Jesus Christ. Despite the localized particularity of his earthly life, as a Jew living briefly in Palestine, Jesus may be known as Savior and Lord by persons of every generation, nationality, culture, language, and social estate. The fact that Christianity has generally been a "Western religion" does not disprove his universality. It has been, and continues to be, demonstrated by Christians in all the world that Jesus Christ is "the same yesterday, today, and for ever." This bold assertion of Hebrews seems by now, at least in our limited experience of time, to have been well vindicated.

While Christ remains the same, however, Christologies have always varied. They have differed within the New Testament, among various church traditions, among schools of theological thought, and within the developing thought of the same person. But in view of our limited knowledge of Jesus Christ, (a knowledge imperfect but still sufficient) it is not astonishing to find such variety. Nor does the diversity necessarily detract from the authenticity of the Christian witness to Jesus Christ as both unique and universal. Just as the recognized differences between the Synoptic accounts and those of Paul, the Fourth Gospel, and Hebrews serve to complement one another instead of standing in mutual antithesis, so the several types of Christology can provide a more adequate picture of Jesus Christ than any one of them can.

But what if the limits of legitimate diversity are overreached? What if two or more ways of thinking about Christ are contradictory rather than complementary? What shall be done when good numbers of faithful and intelligent Christians are sure that others have departed from truth in their thinking and have taught a false conception of the person and work of Christ?

These are not hypothetical questions, of course. They are the ones which have necessarily been raised in the history of the church because of suspected and alleged heresies. "Heresy" is a dreadful word for many Christians today, not because they dread heretical teaching, but because they are most unwilling to condemn any religious view which is sincerely believed. To be sure, many frightful crimes have been committed by Christians in the name of Christ and with the specified intention of defending the faith. But the grim and gruesome specters of Nestorius, Savonarola, Hus, Servetus, and Cranmer do not support the idea that the church need not concern itself any longer with the truth of the gospel. There is no unanimity among the churches generally as to what constitutes heresy on particular doctrines. The sword of excommunication is a dangerous weapon to wield, and fortunately these days it remains in its sheath. Even so, when there are deliberate departures from the standards of constitutive elements of the faith, no matter how sincere the motivation, the expression of charity is not in itself an adequate response. Fortunately, too, in most modern societies we have learned to respect and defend freedom of conscience for all persons and the right to adhere to any religious view or to none at all. But the corollary of this wholesome toleration is not indifference or simple relativism with respect to the truth of the gospel of Jesus Christ. Thus, while regretting the acknowledged excesses in zeal for persecuting alleged heretics in the past, we may continue to hold the conviction that there is a point where legitimate diversity of belief ceases to be a matter of mere variation and becomes a dangerous threat to the integrity of the Christian faith itself.

Although it may often be true that yesterday's heresies are today's orthodoxies, this is not an unalterable and dependable rule. Some of yesterday's heresies continue to be just that. And with respect to no other article of faith is the church so sensitive to heretical teaching than that having to do with Jesus Christ himself.

## DECISIVE DEVIATIONS

The New Testament witnesses to Jesus Christ make it inevitable for Christians to confess in some way both his true humanity and his true divinity. The "raw materials" of Christology in the Bible (as R. H. Fuller calls them) do not dictate a uniform doctrine. But they plainly exclude the spurious ideas which lie beyond either pole of the divine-human scale of being. Neither sheer humanity on one side, nor sheer divinity on the other is permissible.

The pendulum of thought about Christ has oscillated between these poles throughout the history of the church, as well as in the lifetime of particular Christian thinkers. This swinging is tolerable until the pendulum, impelled by a skepticism which cannot endure the paradox, passes beyond the critical point at either end of the arc.

Every textbook of church history describes the struggles and pangs which the Christians of the first five centuries seemed obliged to endure in order to contend for the truth about Jesus Christ. It was not simply as though a strong, orthodox mainstream of faith were occasionally disturbed by the eddies of excess on right and left. The whole church, or at least the reflective and articulate members of it, in the face of religious and philosophical challenge from non-Christians, were groping for concepts adequate to express the reality of the Lord whom they met in the New Testament and in personal faith.

It was not so difficult to show cause why a strictly and exclusively human picture of Jesus of Nazareth was inadequate to the point of being heretical. The party or sect of Ebionites fashioned the general pattern, which has reappeared frequently in history, and especially within the past century of Protestantism and of liberal humanism. One could so interpret the four Gospels as to believe that God found in Jesus the man who pleased him most and therefore adopted him, so to speak, as the special bearer of his will and word. Or one could turn this interpretation completely around and assert that Jesus, being a religious genius of unusual perceptivity, was able to teach the superior way of life so effectively that his hearers, and later his readers, were convinced that he spoke for God. In either case, whether by divine adoption or by eminent endowment, Jesus could be no more than a second Moses with a new law, or else a living exemplar and teacher of the best insights concerning human existence. But in order for this picture to be acceptable to people, the crucifixion of Jesus had to be regarded as just a cruel tragedy, while the evangelists' testimony to his resurrection had to be questioned and rejected along with much of the apostolic preaching of salvation. Long before the era of biblical criticism began, therefore, a wedge was driven between the so-called "Jesus of history and the Christ of faith," to the grave detriment of the doctrine of Christ.

Professor John Knox has proposed the plausible thesis, that whenever the early church faced the issue of Christology—i.e., the humanity and divinity of the Lord—it felt obliged to choose the alternative which stressed Jesus' divinity. The motive for this was ostensibly to secure the veracity of the preaching of salvation. Only a divine savior could rescue a fallen, sinful human race. But however right this intuition may have been, it tended to be expressed at the expense of the equally important understanding, classically formulated by Athanasius: What he did not assume (humanity and human flesh) he could not redeem. Despite the protestations of Ignatius of Antioch and Irenaeus of Lyons concerning the true, historical, and human life of Jesus Christ, and despite the clear intention of confessing "suffered under Pontius Pilate" in the early creed, the church included large numbers who gravitated to far in the direction of espousing his sheer divinity.

Docetism was the general category of belief in which the reality of the Incarnation was displaced by the idea of mere appearance of the Christ-figure. He was a deity or divine emissary wearing the temporary disguise of a man called Jesus.

Gnosticism was the religious system which brought docetism to its most intricate and captivating expression. Abhorring all matter as evil and beyond redemption, the Gnostics could scarcely tolerate a doctrine of the divine Wisdom made real flesh.

While the esoteric schemes for emancipation from earthly corruption through attainment of degrees of divine Gnosis, as taught by Gnosticism, have survived in just a few forms of occultism, the docetic view itself remains today in rather wide currency. Not only is the religion known as Christian Science a repository of docetism, but in the minds of many church members there lies an implicit rejection of incarnation and thus of Jesus' genuine humanity.

Sensing the inadequacy, if not the heresy, of this conception of Jesus Christ's person, many Christians today are attracted, either knowingly or unwittingly, to the idea which was promulgated by the presbyter Arius of Egypt in the fourth century. Although Arianism as an organized movement was forcibly suppressed after the Council of Nicaea in 325, the appeal of its Christology has never disappeared entirely. As the late C. S. Lewis, who had the courage to write boldly clear statements of his faith, wrote in the preface to a translation of *The Incarnation of the Word of God* of Athanasius, the attractiveness of Arianism lay in its reasonable, common-sense portrayals of Jesus Christ, like "one of those 'sensible' synthetic religions which are so strongly recommended today." The human mind has trouble comprehending eternity. Therefore a man's common sense and credulity are strained by the confession of a pretemporal, premundane Son of God, who is coequal with the Father, by whom he was begotten, not made. So the Arians sang their jingles about "the time when he was not" and their ante-Nicene tribe increased. But Arius was apparently as little convinced of Jesus Christ's true divinity as of his humanity. He could not accept the fact that the Jesus who was crucified was in all respects, except in sin, a man like himself or you or me. The Arian Christ was neither Ebionite nor docetic nor orthodox. He was more like the demi-gods of Olympus than the incarnate Lord of Galilee. He was a compromising third force over against the divine-human paradox which most Christians believed.

At Nicaea Arianism was attacked theologically by the young Athanasius and rejected by the great majority of the bishops. After 325 it was orthodox to confess that Jesus Christ was *homoousios*, or consubstantial, with the Father in the unity of the Holy Trinity. But the final ratification of the doctrine of true humanity had to wait another 126 years. Nonetheless it may justly be observed that the Arian type of Christology has remained within the church for all these centuries. It has recurred in much so-called Christian art, from the noble Michaelangelo to Salvador Dali and the popular Warner Sallman (who, to the chagrin of critics and theologians, is popular with no one except the people). Likewise, in common acts of devotion, mainly in Roman Catholicism but also in some precincts of Protestantism, the Arian Christ, who is neither God nor man, proves to be the figure whom many can best think about and adore.

So there still abide docetism, Ebionitism, and Arianism, these three; and the worst of these is a matter of one's judgment. We who think of ourselves as enlightened Christians have a proper distaste for hunting heretics. And when we write our ecumenical conference reports today, we are rightly disinclined to conclude each section with a *damnamus* against all who disagree. Nevertheless, we should not let this Christian restraint prevent our acknowledging that the ante-Chalcedonian struggles against the varieties of christological distortion did indeed serve the purpose of preserving the New Testament gospel for centuries to come. The cost of this grim effort was very high, of course. It was paid out to the debit of charity and personal faith and to the credit of corporate hostility and intellectualism. Only the specialized historians know the dimension of such costs. But we who read their works can sense with dismay how the Christian church was strained and rent by the controversies of the fourth and fifth centuries. It was by no means a lovely history in which the reconciling love of Christ overcame dissensions. But for all the personal vanity and political pretension of the major actors, this tragic drama was motivated by a concern of highest import: to preserve, not a bare proposition about the person of Jesus Christ, but an authentic faith in him as Lord of all things and Savior of mankind.

111

## CHALCEDON: ABSOLUTE OR OBSOLETE?

Within the basilica of St. Euphemia the Martyr in the small
city of Chalcedon, just down the coast from imperial Constantinople, the 529 council fathers, mainly Eastern, gathered to
settle the dispute over Christ's person. It was October in the
year 451, but the controversy had continued for a century and
a half. Books published on the 1,500th anniversary of the
council, notably R. V. Sellers' *The Council of Chalcedon*[1] and
essays edited by Alois Grillmaier and Heinrich Bacht, *Das
Konzil von Chalkedon*,[2] have shown how precarious it is for
the amateur student to reduce the council's agenda to a choice
between black-and-white alternatives. Even apart from the personal and ecclesiastical rivalries and political intrigues in Rome,
Alexandria, Antioch, and Constantinople, a coherent and con-
fessible statement of faith in Jesus Christ had to be extracted
from the welter of unbalanced ideas and allegedly heretical
teachings of Eutyches, Nestorius, and the like. The Alexandrine
Cyril and the Roman Pope Leo were the champions of the
orthodoxy which prevailed.

Rejected by the council was the notion that Jesus Christ, in
order to be both human and divine, really was two persons in
the one man. Rejected also was the belief that he had but one
*physis*, or nature, and this was divine. This was even less acceptable than the earlier proposal of Apollinaris, that Jesus
while being in bodily attributes truly human, nevertheless had
the eternal Word (*Logos*) in the place of a human spirit.

Asserted positively and formally decreed was the doctrine of
the divine and human natures, coexisting in the one person of
Jesus of Nazareth. In respect to God the Father Jesus was *homo-
ousios*, that is, of the very same being. In respect to humanity he

[1] (London: S. P. C. K., 1953).
[2] (Würzburg: Echter-Verlag, 1953-1954).

was also *homo-ousios,* and this was underscored by reference to his birth from the womb of Mary, the *Theotokos,* or bearer of God.

Thus the christological paradox was baldly and bindingly decreed as the only true and permissible faith of the church. Moreover, perhaps to tighten the lines of paradox, the council fathers agreed that after the Incarnation, when the divine Word and the human being became one person, there was neither confusion nor change (*asunchútos, atréptos*) of the two natures, nor could they henceforth be divided or separated (*adiairétos, achorístos*).

All of which language is literally Greek to most Christians today and seems to bear as much resemblance to the apostolic preaching of Christ as do triadic number-games to the Triune God.

One should not pass abrupt judgment upon the decree of Chalcedon, however, until he has studied it carefully and tried mentally to enter into the thought-forms and language of the times. The eminent Orthodox theologian, George Florovsky, has even proposed that no one can understand the Chalcedonian subtleties unless he think and speak in Greek. But if this were so, the vast majority of Christians would be forever excluded from understanding this basic formulation, which the churches of the East and the West have honored as authoritative. The attainment of such theological and philosophical empathy was difficult enough for the Latins of the fifth century. The failure to translate the key Greek words *phúsis, ousía, hypóstasis* and *prósopon* into exact Latin equivalents is notorious. *Natura, substantia,* and *persona* did not quite fit, even though they had become basic to the christological language used ever since Tertullian in the Western tradition.

If the non-Hellenic contemporaries could not rightly grasp the whole meaning of the decree, is there any hope for us twentieth-century Christians? The words "substance" and "nature" have changed radically, due to modern scientific reflection. And psychology in general has given us a concept of "person" or personality which is far different from the ancient idea of the "mask" through which the real being was expressed. Has not Chalcedon, then, become obsolete as a guide to our present thinking about Jesus Christ? Present opinion is divided.

Most are willing to acknowledge that the council served a necessary purpose for its time. It excluded as heretical the teachings of Eutyches and the Nestorians, which imperiled faith in Jesus Christ as effective Savior. So it mitigated and eventually ended the contention within the Eastern Orthodox and Western Latin churches. However, this peace was bought at the cost of further schism in the East. The so-called Monophysite churches, sometimes given the gratuitous name, "Lesser Oriental Churches," were cut off from both Rome and Constantinople. Only now in the present decade, after a millennium and a half, is there evident hope of healing this ancient breach, since discussions have at last revealed that the alleged Monophysitism is more amenable to Orthodoxy than was ever realized.

The Council of Chalcedon must be evaluated, moreover, within the limits of its purpose. That is to say, the council was not convened in order to formulate a complete constitution on the person of Jesus Christ. It met to deal with particular threats to matters within a total Christology; so it cannot be blamed for failing to do what it was never intended to do.

A further point seems often to be neglected when we look to the Chalcedonian decree for light on contemporary questions about Christ. Today we are challenged by the critical missionary task in a world in which, for the most part, people are quite skeptical of any transcendent or metaphysical reality. For many Christians the Incarnation is no longer the burden of a faith

114

to be proclaimed, but a question to be avoided in any religious discussions. Thus has skepticism invaded the church and damaged the nerve of mission. But if witness to Christ in a doubting society is of ascendant importance, what help can come from Chalcedon? Manifestly not very much. Because the question decided in 451 was not posed to the church by doubters or adversaries or even potential converts. The question of *how* Jesus Christ's relation both to God and man could be understood was raised by Christians within the church, in order to allay their own uncertainties. Therefore the decree has had relatively little value for missionary and apologetic purposes. It serves, rather, to guide and enlighten those who have already become Christians and accept in faith *that* Jesus Christ was uniquely related to God and man.

As the standard by which Christology has been guided for fifteen centuries, the decree has probably been more influential than any document written after the books of the New Testament. It has been authoritative for both the Orthodox Churches and the Roman Catholic Church; and the churches which follow the Reformation have either formally acknowledged its authority, or else have paid it due respect. The fine points on which the Chalcedonian theologians seemed rather brashly to have attempted an analysis of Christ's personal identity and makeup may now be elusive for us; e.g., Leo the Great's attempt to show that when Jesus did miracles it was by divine power in him, but when he was tempted it was his human nature; or the ensuing debate on Monothelitism, i.e., whether Jesus had only one will or two.

However, the major point of the decree need be regarded as neither unduly speculative, baffling, nor obsolete. It is the plain affirmation which had been adumbrated at the previous councils of Nicaea and Constantinople and formulated in the ecumenical creed which these two produced. And it is unnecessary to understand Greek to know what is meant. It is this: Insofar as Jesus Christ is known to us, he is known as the one man, born of Mary in Bethlehem, crucified in Jerusalem, and encountered by his followers as the Lord raised from the dead; he is known as a genuine human being, and yet as one to whom the evangelists and apostles could readily apply the highest names of divinity, such as Son of God, Lord (*Kurios* = *ADONAI*) and the fullness of God.

We Christians do not believe this because it is absurd, as Tertullian claimed to do. Nor do we flaunt it before non-Christians as a sheer wonder to be admired or a paradox to cause perplexity.

We confess the message of Jesus Christ as the God-man because upon this foundation rest our ministry of reconciliation, the reality of worship, and the existence of the church.

### THE DESIRE FOR RESTATEMENT

Probably few theologians would now maintain that the Chalcedonian decree *invariata* stands as an adequate statement of Christology, although the Orthodox teachers would be less disposed than any others to tamper with it. Friederich Schleiermacher may have been the first of the major theologians to reject the terms of the decree. But when there is a call to reject or revise the words and concepts of Chalcedon, we must ask whether the reality to which these refer is also being rejected or revised. Contemporary theologians so different as Emil Brunner, Edmund Schlink, Paul Tillich, and Hans Küng have clearly suggested that a new vocabulary is needed to replace the key words of the decree. But they are not thereby dismissing the content of it. (However, it is at least questionable whether Tillich remains as true to the Chalcedonian Christology as he promised to be in his *Systematic Theology*.) In a series of lectures on this subject Albert C. Outler advanced the motto,

116

"Back to Chalcedon—and forward!" This is a most valuable directive for both christological reflection and the proclamation of the gospel today.

Outright rejection of the decree would be tantamount to the acceptance of either one of the ancient heresies: either the humanistic extreme or else some form of docetism.

Feeling the need to express the complete unity of Jesus Christ, Schleiermacher bluntly discarded the concept of the two natures in his person.[3] In place of this he endeavored to construct a Christology on the idea of Jesus' perfect "God-consciousness." More than any other man, for reasons which cannot be known, Jesus had a prodigious ability to know the will of God and to feel intimate communion with him. Schleiermacher claimed that this was not just the subjective experience of Jesus, but that the "God-consciousness" was the very power of God at work in him. Therein lay the peculiar character of his relation to God; and therefore Jesus was the uniquely perfect man. This was not a question of ontological speculation, as he considered Chalcedon's statement to be, but of God's endowing and empowering Jesus with what he called the "dignity" requisite to his work as redeemer of mankind. Schleiermacher is not easy to understand here. He does try to retain the singular character of Jesus' person. But it is difficult to see how this "God-consciousness," which might be deemed the equivalent of his divinity, is a gift in which other human beings with varying degrees of such consciousness could not also participate.

The influence of Schleiermacher has been very extensive, of course. And after the rough attacks upon him by his two cultured despisers, Karl Barth and Emil Brunner in their younger years, there is now a movement to rehabilitate his theology. Yet, it remains at best dubious whether a return to what is

[3] *The Christian Faith* (Naperville, Ill.: Alec R. Allenson, 1928), Proposition 95.

generally seen as a subjectivistic basis for Christology will satisfy either the Christian's craving to understand Jesus Christ or his need to know how to articulate the gospel to others.

Although Schleiermacher commanded the nineteenth century in Protestantism, the influence of Albrecht Ritschl upon some German and much Anglo-Saxon theology was particularly strong. The key word of his interpretation of Christianity was "moral value," which none would contest as a worthy concept. The latter half of the century was a time of increasing emphasis upon the teaching of Jesus and decreasing concern with the question of who he was. Therefore, for many of the time the Ritschlian dictum concerning Jesus was definitive: Jesus had the value of God. This concept, as illuminated by the words and deeds of Jesus in the Gospels, certainly was applicable as a guide to Christian life. In this respect it had a clear advantage over what seemed to be the abstract intellectualism of the traditional christological teaching. And yet Ritschl really failed to come to terms with the essential and perennial question, Who is Jesus Christ? His teaching of "moral value" was vulnerable to loose interpretation. As appropriated by some Christians, it degenerated to the level of the banal humanistic portrait of Jesus as the best of all good men.

Recently prevailing over traditional norms has been the provocative idea of the "New Being" as set forth by Paul Tillich. He must surely be admired for his prodigious effort to make Christian theology amenable and intelligible to contemporary intellectuals, especially those who have explored the meaning of human life by way of depth psychology and the philosophy of existentialism. But Tillich did not invent the concept of New Being for this purpose. It is as old as Paul's letters.

Although the ancient Paul did not carefully describe what he meant by the "new creation" in Christ, he asserted, with more

118

emphasis on Resurrection than Incarnation, that in Jesus Christ was effected the beginning of the really renewed humanity. And this could happen within the sphere of human history only because of who Jesus Christ was and is: the eternal Son who emptied himself in order to become man and assume the form of a servant, even to the point of death by crucifixion, so that he could be raised and exalted as the one New Man. Thus, when any man by faith has entered into full communion with Christ, there is a new creation.

The contemporary Paul also sees this New Being in Jesus Christ. But Tillich is apparently even more cautious than Paul in explaining precisely what he means. Why is Jesus as the Christ called the New Being? Because he alone has somehow overcome the dreadful bane of man's life, namely, the tragic estrangement between his essence and his existence. All persons in this earthly life suffer from the brokenness and partiality inherent in existence. Only Jesus as the Christ experienced the genuine and authentic life; so only he is qualified to be the healer of man's fragmented, inauthentic existence.

This is an appealing and apparently satisfying interpretation of Christian faith for many of Tillich's readers, and one would not wish to contradict their expressions of appreciation for it. However, his Christology still leaves the reader wondering who this Jesus as the Christ really was and is, and how he alone can be the New Being for all persons. It may well be suggested that Tillich's valuable thought here would be strengthened and clarified if place were given for the concepts of the Chalcedonian decree.

Dietrich Bonhoeffer's Christology differs greatly from Tillich's, but his chief concern was the same. He felt a passion to make Jesus Christ known to men and women who have forfeited the "God-hypothesis" in all their thinking and belief. For this widely approved reason Bonhoeffer's designation of Jesus as "the man for others" has gained much currency. This is a description which is surely true to the New Testament portrayal of Jesus' life in a way more profoundly meaningful than Ritschl's. And it is quite pertinent to the increasing numbers of people today who are sensitive to the lovelessness, loneliness, frustration, and suffering of their fellow men. However, it would be a travesty to conclude that Bonhoeffer was content to commend a merely human and humanitarian Jesus. His lectures and writings on Christology, posthumously collected and published, give strong affirmation of the substance of the perennial doctrine of Christ. Along with the designation of the lowly "man for others," he spoke clearly of the transcendent Word as embodied in Jesus Christ. Making a pun, but not for humor, he said, "Christology is Logology." To know Jesus Christ is to know the divine Logos. But can we fully know the meaning and mystery of his person? Bonhoeffer is more modest than Chalcedonian fathers were, for he admits that God alone knows this mystery. And he is less sanguine than his Lutheran ancestor in confession, Philip Melanchthon, concerning the way we come to know within necessary limits just who Christ was and is. In his oft-quoted dictum Melanchthon declared that knowing who Jesus Christ is depends on first knowing his benefits or his redeeming work. In technical terms soteriology must precede Christology. But not for Bonhoeffer: "Only when I know who does this work, do I have access to the work of Christ," he said.[4] The self-giving life for others, the willingness to be despised and rejected, the disturbing and inspiring teaching, and the death on the cross—all of these depend upon the personal identity of Jesus Christ before they can of their intrinsic worth be called redemptive. This is why the doctrine of the unity of the divine and human in him takes precedence

[4] *Wer ist und wer war Jesus Christus* (Hamburg: Furche Verlag, 1962), p. 24.

over interpretations of atonement and reconciliation. Even as the man for others, Jesus remains the unique and universal man. With great men such as Goethe and Socrates, said Bonhoeffer, we can have encounter and dialogue, and upon this depends our education and ethos. But upon our encounter with Jesus Christ depends our life and death.[5]

Christian thinkers must necessarily obey the restless impulse to seek words and phrases which will express with all possible clarity what the church has always known to be true of Jesus Christ: the singularity of his person and the comprehensiveness of his saving life. Neither a simple "back to the Bible" nor a "back to Chalcedon" attitude will suffice, even though both Bible and Chalcedon and the long tradition of expounding the gospel of Jesus Christ are indispensable. As efforts are made to find the fitting and meaningful words, excesses and errors are to a degree inevitable. But they are worth risking, even at the cost of occasional heretical utterance, because the church's doctrine cannot remain static and immutable. Christ is the same yesterday, today, and forever, precisely because he is knowable to human beings of all times and all places, from the primitive to the richly cultured, from the illiterate to the highly sophisticated, from Jerusalem and Samaria to the ever receding boundaries of human experience.

[5] *Ibid.,* p. 19.

# 6

## THE FINALITY OF CHRIST IN A
## WHITEHEADIAN PERSPECTIVE

### I

The finality of Jesus Christ is first a historical question. It is my conviction that in our day we can affirm this finality only if we can make historical sense out of this claim. To make historical sense out of this claim one must write some kind of universal history in which the central and decisive role of Jesus Christ is made to appear. I can here offer only an outline sketch of such a history.

My purpose is to address myself to the christological problem from a Whiteheadian perspective. Since I do think from this perspective, this is a thoroughly congenial task. On the other hand, the relation between Whitehead's philosophy and a sketch of universal history is neither simple nor obvious. Hence, I shall preface my outline of the sketch with a few remarks on the approach to history to which I am led by my Whiteheadian perspective. I will present the relevant points simply as a series of theses without attempting any justification.

First, only individual entities are actual. Statements about groups or societies of individuals must always be related finally to particular individuals.

Second, all individual entities are subjects. There is no such thing as an actual entity that is merely an object.

Third, all individual subjects are momentary in duration. Each is an actual occasion of experience which is to be thought of neither as infinitesimal nor as extended through any considerable period of time.

Fourth, all actual entities have certain common structural characteristics. This means that ontologically there are important identities between an occasion of human experience and an occasion of electronic experience.

Fifth, within the context of these identities there are vast differences among the actual entities.

Sixth, every occasion takes account of its past, but the way in which it does so is finally its own decision. That is, one of the features common to all actual entities is the influence upon them of all that is in their past. A second feature common to all actual entities is that the influence of the past upon them does not amount to total determination of their own self-actualization.

From these ontological principles I draw the following conclusions about history.

First, there is no strictly ontological distinction between history and nature. We cannot erect any distinction between historical events and natural events into an absolute duality.

Second, there are in fact great differences between historical events and natural events. The amount of similarity and the types of dissimilarity are to be worked out in detail and not from any a prioristic position.

Third, differences of major importance are to be found among natural events and among historical events as well as between natural events in general and historical events in general.

Fourth, this means that there are differences among human occasions of experience that are almost as great as the differences between human occasions in general and subhuman occasions in general.

Fifth, history is ultimately the history of subjects in their subjectivity and not the account of events externally viewed or reconstructed.

Sixth, the kind of existence known to any given subject depends chiefly upon his particular past as that is embodied in his culture. This means that man is primarily formed by history.

Seventh, the most important subject of historical inquiry is the emergence of new forms of existence. If it can be claimed historically that Jesus Christ is final, this must mean that the mode of existence given in him stands in peculiar relation to all other modes of existence.

I should add that I do not suppose that the understanding of history in which Jesus appears as final is one that is neutral or objective. I assume that only the Christian sees history in this way. However, this does not mean that the Christian experiences himself as imposing some special interpretation upon resistant data. Rather, the Christian finds this the most adequate and illuminating understanding of the data. To him it seems that it is rather the non-Christian historian, with his tendency to belittle the historical centrality of the Christ-event, who distorts the historical material with which he works. The problem of perspective is a universal one. Our concern should be to attain a genuinely adequate perspective rather than a generally accepted one. The claim that this genuinely adequate perspective is given us in Jesus Christ is another formulation of the claim that Jesus Christ is final.

At this point I turn to my outline of a sketch of the history of human existence.

I assume that the transition from animal to human existence was a gradual one and that if we had before us today all the creatures who followed each other in this evolutionary development, we could not draw any clear line between those we would call subhuman and those we would call human. On the other hand, my impression of the evolutionary process is that from time to time fateful thresholds are crossed that lead rather rapidly to dramatic new forms.

The threshold whose crossing it is best to associate with the emergence of man is that of language. Man shares consciousness and intelligence, in the sense of the ability to learn from experience, with much of the animal world. Rationality in the sense of a distinctively human faculty depends upon language but is far more restricted. It depends upon a marriage of intelligence and language that played a minor role among precivilized men. In its origins language probably functioned primarily in the service of the unconscious rather than as a means of improving man's technical control or rational communication. The symbolizations expressed in the language of primitive men even today are hardly intelligible as means of pragmatic adjustment to the environment.

The emergence of reason is roughly to be correlated with the rise of civilization. Prior to this point, I suggest, the superior intelligence of man in relation to animals and the peculiar characteristics of his physiology can explain his superior achievements without reference to any major role of language. But the kind of division of labor and organization involved in civilization requires a high level of rationality. Language was brought into the service of intelligence. Consciousness thereby achieves considerable autonomy in relation to the unconscious.

It would be tedious to repeat at every point in this sketch that the transformations of existence to which I refer occur gradually. I do not mean that there was at one point a precivilized human community in which language served exclusively for symbolization of meanings controlled by the unconscious

125

and that there then suddenly emerged another in which large segments of life were controlled by reason. Probably from very early times there were important flashes of reason and sometimes relatively sustained uses of language in the service of intelligence. Equally within the great cities of antiquity there were undoubtedly myriads of individuals in whose lives reason played a very small role. Nevertheless, corresponding to the social, economic, political, and technological contrasts between primitive, tribal life and Egyptian or Mesopotamian civilization, we must posit a radical change in the kind of existence known to the individual.

The difference can be described in terms of myth. By myth I mean language in the service of unconscious symbolization. In this respect it resembles dreams. Although many of the actions of precivilized man expressed intelligence, his verbal accounts of these intelligent actions were not characteristically rational. His world of meanings was pervasively mythological. In the ancient civilizations mythological meanings remained dominant, but in certain areas of life rational meanings asserted themselves with great effectiveness.

From the point of view of the history of existence the next great transition is that in which influential men appeared who insisted on rationalizing the system of meanings by which men lived. I assume that this could not have occurred until reason had demonstrated its powers in ever-widening areas of life, and I also assume that those who undertook to rationalize the meanings by which men lived were still deeply influenced by unconscious meanings. Nevertheless, we have here one of the really great turning points of universal history.

I am describing in my own way what Karl Jaspers and Lewis Mumford describe as the Axial Period of history. Jaspers shows that between 800 and 200 B.C. man entered a new phase of his historical existence in China, India, Persia, Palestine, and

Greece. He holds that the kind of existence that there arose is still fundamentally our existence today, that the problems then raised and the types of answers then considered still constitute the context within which we wrestle with basic human problems.

I am persuaded that Jaspers is very nearly correct and that his insight is extremely important for our understanding of our present situation of a common worldwide history. Nevertheless, I believe that his presentation (and that of Mumford as well) is misleading in crucial respects.

First, by correctly emphasizing the remarkable parallels between the several separate developments from archaic to axial man, Jaspers leaves the impression that their differences are relatively unimportant. Second, by emphasizing how we still live in the context established by axial man, he underestimates the significant developments that have taken place within this context as they affect our basic existence. Since Jaspers' failure in these two respects prevents the crucial question of the finality of Jesus from receiving an appropriate context of discussion, I take it as my task to show both that there are major differences in the forms of existence known to the several axial peoples and that at least in the case of Jesus, developments of utmost importance for human existence occurred after 200 B.C. In doing this, I consider myself to be supplementing rather than contradicting Jaspers' basic insight.

My view is that all the axial peoples shifted the seat of existence from the unconscious to the conscious. All of them rationalize their received symbol systems. For all of them this meant an entirely new mode of existence bringing quite new kinds of problems and possibilities. Yet each of these peoples moved into this new existence by asking quite different questions and by rationalizing in quite different ways. Hence the modes of existence into which they entered, while parallel and

127

roughly equal in depth and power, were qualitatively quite diverse. I can only try to remind you of these differences by reference to three of them: the Indian, the Greek, and the Hebrew.

In India axial man turned from the attempt to manipulate the outer conditions of life by magical incantation to the attempt to know and save himself in his inwardness. He was convinced that success in the outer world was ultimately futile, that it left man in an endless cycle of existence in which every pleasure is but the prelude to pain and the whole succession is without meaning. Indeed, his critical reflection persuaded him that the whole outer world is only the world that appears, and that reality must be sought in some other way than through the senses. As he turned inward into his own subjectivity, he found that that, too, in all its particularity belongs to the world of appearance. The ultimate subject of his own experience, the self or Atman, is wholly undifferentiated and unindividualized. The realization that the true self is unaffected by the endless flux of the phenomenal world is the goal of much Indian thought and life, for through it man achieves freedom from the suffering of the world.

I realize that at best I have spoken of only one of the great Indian schools. Yet I think that it is typical and that in important respects all of them move in the same direction. All of them turn inward in their quest for reality and release, and all of them believe that this reality is other than the differentiated and individuated existence of the ordinary consciousness.

The Greek development, despite its occasional points of contact with Indian thought, is fundamentally different. The fundamental effort of axial man in Greece was to order his world rather than to transcend it. This order was achieved in the first instance aesthetically. The terrible and fascinating mythical powers were transformed into beautiful and intelligible

128

persons who were objectified and distanced for admiring contemplation. This freed everyday life and reflection to become open to nature and man as they are given in sense experience, and especially in vision. Personal excellence had to do in large measure with the excellence of the appearance to others of the man in question, both in the sense of physical beauty and of excellence of action.

Within this context of an aesthetically distanced world, reason as such came into its own. The detachment of aesthetic contemplation allows one to be formed in his experience by the forms that are present in the objects themselves rather than imposing meanings upon them from one's previous experience or unconscious needs. This contemplation of form made possible in its turn reflection upon forms, the attempt to conform thought to pattern found objectively in it. The brilliant achievements of Greece in mathematics, philosophy, and natural science are the amazement of the world. Finally, the achievements of reason led to reflection about reason itself and to a prizing of reason as such that is likewise peculiarly Greek. For one major segment of Greek thought human excellence came to be defined as excellence of rationality. The ideal man was the perfectly rational man.

The problem of abrupt characterization is even more acute with the Greeks than with the Indians because the Greek achievement was one which encouraged a more radical internal diversity than the Indian. The understanding of rationality among those who prized it varied greatly. Others protested against reason in the name of pleasure. Still others revolted more radically and sought to regain wholeness at the level of the unconscious in Dionysian orgies. Nevertheless, for schematic purposes it is helpful to think of the Greek achievement in terms of the formal ordering of the world, first by aesthetic distancing, and then in terms of rational speculative reflection.

The understanding of man that accompanied this development was likewise one that approved aesthetic and rational excellence.

The Hebrews carried with them into their axial period ideas about deity that were left behind by both Indians and Greeks. Ideas about divine lawgivers and covenants between men and gods can be found in the primitive mythologies of many peoples, but in most cases the transition to the axial period involved the rejection of such mythical thinking. Among the Hebrews, in contrast, the axial development consisted in the ethicizing and historicizing of such thinking rather than its rejection. The process of axial transformation was constituted initially by reflection about the tribal deity, a reflection in which Yahweh came to be understood as the personal creator of heaven and earth who acted in history to reveal to man his righteous will. In interaction with this God, man also discovered himself as a person with responsibility to obey. He became aware of himself in his inwardness as he knew himself to be known of God. And he came to understand that finally he stood before God as an individual man and not only as a part of a covenant community.

For the Indian the great central image is that of the relation of appearance and reality; the phenomenal flux on the one hand and the abiding subject on the other. For the Greek the crucial categories are found in the forms apprehended in visual experience and the relations among them. For the Hebrew existence came to be in the I-Thou encounter with God that brought into being a kind of personhood that was also capable of I-thou relations with other men.

In basic respects this prophetic understanding of existence became a fixed part of Israel's peculiar life. For some it was closely associated with expectation of the earthly triumph of the righteous, an expectation doomed to continual frustration by the actual course of history. The growing antithesis between what was and what should be led to the transformation of the prophetic hope into an apocalyptic hope. The vindication of the righteous refused by history is still assured by the justice of God, but now by a wholly supernatural overcoming of history. For others the individualistic elements in the prophetic message allowed for an understanding of the vindication of the righteous in terms of individual judgment after death. Here the tension between the *is* and the *ought* is relaxed just enough to require men to come to terms with the conditions of possibility in actual social life, although their dealings there are to be guided not by considerations of prudence within that context, but by the demand of God presented in the law.

Apocalypticism and Pharisaism are both legitimate children of prophetism. The former maintains the extremism of the prophets, the refusal to accept the occurrences of history as a measure of the true reality, and the insistence on the ultimate victory of God. Pharisaism, on the other hand, maintains the prophetic concern for righteousness in the here and now and understands much better than apocalypticism that each individual stands responsible before God.

For both apocalypticism and Pharisaism God is experienced in his absence. For Pharisaism the presence of God to history is primarily in the past; for apocalypticism, in the future. Whereas the prophets had known God in his immediate presence to them in judgment and, to a lesser extent, in grace, the Pharisees identified God's will with the law. In so doing they absolutized a mixture of prophetic and archaic principles and treated this mixture as beyond critical analysis. The apocalypticists refused to any existing reality such sacred authority and absolutized instead a future state. But both failed to maintain the purity of the prophetic vision in which God alone is sacred or absolute.

Jesus appears in this context as a new prophet. Yet he does not represent only the revival of prophetism. He is like the prophets in his sense of God's absolute presence to him, but he goes beyond the prophets in his claim of personal authority. He speaks out of his own existence as that is formed in his personal knowledge of God rather than as a spokesman for the message entrusted him by God.

As a new prophet Jesus is also the consummation and transformation of both apocalypticism and Pharisaism. As an apocalypticist he proclaims the coming of the kingdom in such a way that in the very proclamation the kingdom itself is brought near. As a Pharisee he proclaims the absolute demand of God for human righteousness in such a sense that the law itself is transcended and set aside. In the radical intensification of the essential genius of each, Jesus brings into being a mode of existence that fulfills the central thrust of prophetism in a way that is fundamentally unsurpassable.

This then is the direction in which I believe the finality of Jesus within the context of the Hebraic achievement is to be understood. Jesus shows us radically what it means to exist from God and for God. We are incapable of imagining any more complete embodiment of this mode of existence, and certainly history has offered us none to date. Where we find the closest approximations to this achievement we find also those who most emphasize their dependence on Jesus and their remoteness from reproducing his existence. While we cannot assert as historians that Jesus' achievement will not be matched in the future, it is virtually certain that any approximation to such matching will show his influence. Hence this possibility does not challenge the finality of Jesus.

These claims are, of course, seriously disputed by Jews (and Moslems) who are also heirs of the prophetic tradition. I cannot carry on here a discussion of their counterclaims. I do believe that the major reasons for continuing rejection of the finality of Jesus by Judaism (and perhaps also by Islam) are to be found in two areas, both essentially extraneous to the claim I am making. First, the behavior of Christians, and especially their behavior toward Jews, has made openmindedness toward the claim of Jesus exceedingly difficult for the Jew. Second, the doctrine of Jesus' deity, however it may be explained by sophisticated theologians, is necessarily an affront to Jews and, indeed, also to many others. How Judaism will react to the claim of Jesus when it can view this claim without pressure from the sanctions and violence of a "Christian" majority and dissociated from metaphysical dogmas about him, remains to be seen.

The crucial question is that of the relation of Jesus to those modes of human existence attained in other axial transformations. It is far more difficult to claim that Jesus is the fulfillment of Indian or Greek existence. Yet something can and must be said here, too.

In the case of the Greek achievement we are not condemned simply to speculation. The great success of Christianity was among persons who were heirs of Greek civilization. Furthermore, on the whole the Greeks carried with them into their new Christian faith a continuing positive appreciation of their Greek heritage. They experienced Christianity as the consummation and transformation of their existence.

Against this rather obvious reading of history two important objections can be raised, and even in this very brief compass I accept some responsibility to indicate how I would counter them. First, it is possible to view the Christianity of the Hellenistic world as more fundamentally a product of that world than a result of the impact of the Jewish Jesus. In this case the victory of Christianity is simply another step in the evolution or devolution of the religious life of Greek civilization. It represents an absorption of Jewish elements into that civilization but not a transformation or completion by a fundamentally new principle introduced from without. My response to this is that despite the immense influence of Hellenistic culture upon Christianity the fundamental institutional, liturgical, and ethical patterns that won out in the struggle within the church are better understood in terms of their Hebraic background than in terms of their Hellenistic background. More important, the canonization of the Old and New Testaments represented the victory of the Hebraic side of the spiritual struggle and insured that progressively its peculiar thrust would play a larger rather than a smaller role in the general self-understanding of Christendom.

Second, one may well argue that although the Hebraic development as consummated in Jesus won out over the decadent Hellenism of the first and second centuries, this tells us nothing of its relationship to that healthy Hellenism of the classical period. From this point of view it may be claimed that the mentality embodied in the great philosophers is more comprehensively adequate and offers a more final resting place for the human spirit than anything that has come out of Israel. Even if this is not true in just the form in which reason expressed itself in Plato and Aristotle, the philosophical program to which they gave brilliant expression and profound impulse stands beyond Jesus and finally in judgment upon him. Even if Jesus shows us what it means to live from God and for God, only philosophical reason can judge whether that kind of existence is based upon reality or illusion. In this case, whatever happened eighteen or nineteen centuries ago, it is in principle the rational, critical, reflective spirit of the Greeks that paves the way for the supreme achievement of mankind rather than Jesus.

Against this extremely important criticism of the claim for the finality of Jesus a very complex and thorough counterargument is required. I can here only indicate the directions such an argument must take. It must show both the dependence of rational activity on something more fundamental than itself and the intrinsic limits of reason. I would argue, on the one hand, that participation in Christian existence liberates the reason to its fullest freedom and, on the other hand, that reason by itself can establish nothing whatsoever with respect to the meaning and purpose of existence.

We turn now to the kind of claim that can be made for the finality of Jesus in relation to the Indian achievement. Here too we must take note of a strong and persuasive counterclaim that it is in Indian religion and philosophy that Western existence must find its completion. In the discussion of the contributions of the East and of the West to the coming world civilization it is often proposed that whereas the West can contribute its technology, the East, and especially India, must provide the spiritual wisdom.

The argument for Indian superiority can be briefly outlined. According to this view Jesus is recognized as a truly great spiritual teacher. It is even possible to accept the view that he is true revelation of God and even Son of God. However, the Western mind has made of this correct interpretation an exclusive claim which is inevitably unacceptable to others who have found God in other forms. Indian thinkers, in contrast, have recognized the plurality of forms in which the holy power manifests itself to man and the plurality of ways in which men of diverse gifts and temperaments can and should approach God. Thus Indian thought can give ample place for the whole Christian experience without excluding others, whereas Christians are unable to be equally open to other manifestations of God and paths to salvation.

The claim for the superiority of Indian thought is a serious one with great appeal also in the West. Christians must listen carefully and recognize the truth in the criticism of their all too often condemnatory and imperialistic attitude toward other religions. Nevertheless, Christians must also respond by re-formulating and reaffirming their claim of the finality of Jesus if not of their own form of belief and existence.

There is first the low-level historical fact that in the inter-action between Western and Indian culture the dominant in-fluence in the life of the spirit has thus far been from West to East. This might, of course, simply mean that technological superiority involved some kind of compulsion upon the Indian mind to accept also other dimensions of influence, but I think this can be shown to be a superficial view. Few leaders of contemporary India would wish to give up the kind of humanism and humanitarianism which in recent times has been developing under Western influence. They prefer instead to see this as a natural development of their own tradition and to belittle the contribution of the West to its emergence. Likewise, if India is to survive in the modern world, she must enter into a con-cern for history that is far more Hebraic than Indian in its origins. Or again, the understanding of the relation of man and nature that underlies technology and its effective applica-tion to the problems of life involves the spiritual dimension of man. In the West the appropriate spiritual climate was formed by a synthesis of Greek and Hebraic achievements in which I have argued that the Hebraic in its peculiarly Christian form was the controlling principle. As India moves increasingly toward the incorporation into her total life of Western tech-nology she must also adopt and adapt elements from the Western synthesis.

These highly pragmatic considerations are, of course, not decisive. The discussion needs to be conducted at another level, the level of the relation of the modes of existence of the two communities. Here it is my thesis that the mode of existence formed in the I-Thou relation to God is able to transform and fulfill the mode of existence to which Indian spiritual inwardness and mysticism has led. Without denying or belittling the value of the serenity and compassion in which Indian religion at its best eventuates, the Christian can and must affirm that the richly personal existence that fulfills itself in love for the neighbor can incorporate the values of Indian existence in a still higher synthesis.

Early in this chapter I noted that I could not suppose that the view of history in which the finality of Jesus Christ appears is a neutral or impartial one. This view of history is given to one who sees history in a perspective already formed by Jesus Christ. It is finally a confession rather than an argument, although a great many arguments may go into its self-explanation. Hence, I do not at all suppose that I or any one else can by critical description alone win all intelligent and rational men to the acknowledgment of Jesus' finality.

On the other hand, I do believe very strongly in the potential value of such an account. I believe that the encounter with Jesus has or can have on many persons an extremely potent effect that is often inhibited or dissipated by their inability to adopt formulations of Jesus' finality that they have been led to suppose are essential to its existential acceptance. The task of apologetics must at least be that of the removal of unnecessary stumbling blocks.

In this connection I am increasingly persuaded that we must radically dissociate, at least initially, the finality of Jesus and the Christian church. The Christian church certainly witnesses to that finality, but we should not suppose that the acknowledgment of that finality must necessarily involve identification with any existing Christian institution. Perhaps the next phase of the historical vindication of the finality of Jesus may not involve further extension of the institutional church. Perhaps it may be instead that Hindus, without ceasing to be Hindus, will find in Jesus the fulfillment of Hinduism. If so Hinduism will also be transformed. In such a transformation, I am convinced, many features of Western Christianity would be duplicated or paralleled, but certainly not all. And we should not suppose that we of the West have the wisdom to discriminate the aspects of our form of Christianity that are universal in character.

# II

There is a second dimension to the claim of the finality of Jesus. From the very beginning Christians have affirmed that God was present to and in Jesus in a preeminent way. Furthermore, Christians have believed that this presence of God to and in Jesus involved the distinctive initiative of God and was not simply a function of the peculiar virtue of this man.

The theological problems to which this conviction has given rise are notorious. When we affirm the primacy of the divine initiative in determining the divine presence, the genuine humanity of Jesus becomes doubtful. He appears more as a vessel or puppet than as a truly human person. On the other hand, the insistence on his full humanity tends to imply that God's presence was a consequence of Jesus' acts in relation to God and to his fellow man, that any man who acts as Jesus acted would know the same presence.

The church has officially rejected both the curtailment of the primacy of the divine initiative and the limitation of Jesus' full humanity. Christians have been convinced that what happened in Jesus cannot be explained simply as the result of the excellence of one human will. On the other hand, they have insisted that the human freedom and responsibility must not be denied. My belief is that here the church has shown sound judgment and that it is our task to maintain the dual affirmation.

Given this duality there are two possible approaches. One may start with the act of God and attempt to understand the humanity secondarily, or one may start with the full humanity and attempt to understand how God acted on and in that person. Roughly, these are the approaches of Alexandria and of Antioch. The creeds represent a compromise between these, but the typical orthodox interpretations of the creeds are Alexandrine. This Alexandrine victory expresses itself most clearly in the doctrine of the impersonal humanity of Jesus.

I believe this Alexandrine victory to have been exceedingly unfortunate, and I deplore its implied perpetuation in the slogan of the World Council of Churches. The Antiochenes were far more faithful to the Bible in their insistence on recognizing the fully personal humanity of Jesus. They lost out in part because they had available to them no conceptuality for explaining how God could at his own initiative be genuinely present to and in a man without displacing some element in the personal humanity of that man. The philosophy of Alfred North Whitehead offers us at this point new possibilities that have not yet been sufficiently explored. Hence the rest of this section is devoted to an attempt to indicate briefly how from a Whiteheadian perspective a Christian can affirm the special presence of God to and in a man without reducing the man's full personal responsible humanity on the one hand or minimizing the divine initiative on the other.

Whitehead's language is not easy, and this difficulty is rooted in the fact that his vision of reality differs markedly from that which, in spite of the twentieth-century scientific revolution, is still the common sense of Western man. Hence I must make a brief attempt to invite you into the strange new world of Whitehead's vision.

In the first sentence of his greatest work, *Process and Reality*, Whitehead wrote, "These lectures are based upon a recurrence to that phase of philosophic thought which began with Descartes and ended with Hume." This tradition was one which began with the immediately given human experience as the basis for all reflection and all understanding of whatever is. It is, thus, subjectivist. The clue to reality is first and foremost experience itself in its full subjectivity. Whitehead shares this subjectivism.

However, the subjectivist tradition culminating in Hume regarded the data of experience as being qualities and qualities only. This leads in all consistency to solipsism, for if all that is given to the experiencing subject is qualities, he can have no basis for arriving at any notion of other entities than himself. Whitehead appeals to the fact that all of us are absolutely certain that our experience in any given moment does not exhaust reality, as indicating that the real data of our experience are not qualities but other entities. This modification of the subjectivist tradition causes Whitehead to characterize his position as a reformed subjectivism.

The only clue that we can have as to the nature of these other entities that we are constantly experiencing is our own experience. Hence Whitehead speculates that like ourselves they are actual occasions of experience. "Actual occasion of experience" is his technical term for the final individual entities which alone are fully actual. Everything else is either an aspect of such an occasion or a society of such occasions. Thus, the real individual things are all subjects, and each subject has as its data other subjects.

This statement needs to be qualified in one respect. An occasion of experience occurs in a moment and then is past. In the moment of its occurrence it enjoys subjectivity, but when it is past, that subjectivity is past, too. It is always as past that a subject functions as the datum for another subject, and such a past subject may properly be called an object. This means that the fundamental mode of real relationship is that in which an occasion of experience has as its data objects that are past occasions of experience. This relationship Whitehead calls a prehension. Every real, direct relationship between men or between man and God is a prehension. If we are to understand what it must mean to speak of a relation between a man and God, we must grasp what is involved in a prehension.

The example of a prehension most readily accessible for reflection is the relation of a momentary occasion of human experience to a predecessor occasion. Consider for example your own experience in the moment in which I finish this sentence and the immediately preceding occasion of your experience. There is, I assume, an immense amount of continuity. Most of what you were feeling in the earlier moment you were feeling in the latter. This continuity did not depend upon conscious recall of the earlier experience by the latter. Rather it seems to flow into the latter, almost to continue itself in the latter. The high degree of this continuity was a function in part of the preceding occasion which, we will suppose, intended that an attitude of attention would be continued, and partly of the subsequent occasion which reaffirmed the intention to be attentive. Most of the meanings present in the earlier occasion recurred in the latter. Thus there was massive continuity of feeling and meaning between the two occasions.

In Whitehead's view we cannot speak of this simply as a continuation. The later moment of experience is a new experience, however similar it may be to the earlier. What is given in one occasion, if it is to be present also in the later occasion, must be reenacted there. The extent to which that reenaction occurs is determined partly by the earlier occasion and partly by the later one. For example, in the earlier moment you might have decided to shut me off because what I have to say is not worth attending to. In that case there would be much less reenactment in the subsequent occasion of the feelings (perhaps

141

of strain and annoyance) that had characterized the preceding experience. On the other hand, such a decision made in one moment might in a split second be reversed, so that the new occasion would after all reenact much of the experience of its predecessors.

When we are considering the weight of the influence of the earlier occasion on the later, we may speak of causal efficacy. Every occasion has causal efficacy for its successors. That means that in every moment of my experience I cannot help but be influenced by my past. I cannot choose not to be the person who has had those past experiences or to be now as if I had not had those experiences. However, it is very important to understand also what is *not* meant by causal efficacy. Causal efficacy does not mean that the past determines just *how* I will be influenced by it in the present. For example, in the illustration I gave before, your experience in the moment you reversed your decision to stop listening was clearly not determined by the previous decision to stop listening, but the experience in that moment was still quite different from what it would have been if the earlier decision had not occurred. The later occasion is necessarily affected by the earlier, but the way in which it is affected is by no means settled by the character of the earlier occasion. Causal efficacy is real but not totally determinative.

Viewed from the side of the new experience, the matter may be put as follows. The new experience must prehend all its predecessors. They jointly constitute its initial data. But it may select from the total richness of the initial data as to the aspects of their experience that it will reenact. These aspects become its objective data, that is, by these selected qualities it objectifies its initial data, and only in this selected way are these past experiences allowed to become actively effective in the new occasion. The principle of selection is the subjective aim of the new occasion, that is, the conscious or unconscious purpose that guides it to the attainment of some definite outcome.

I have been speaking of the relation of a momentary occasion of human experience to its predecessor. I selected this because we can think of this relation more easily than of any other. But we must remember that this is only one instance of a prehension. All real relations in the universe, from the electronic level to the divine are prehensions and are to be understood in fundamentally the same way. Every new occasion must take account of the past by reenacting it in some way, but just how it reenacts the past is never wholly determined by that past. Thus the past has causal efficacy for the future, and this explains the massive continuity in nature, but the present always determines just how that past will be effective, and this explains the spontaneity, unpredictability, life, and mentality, that are also real factors in the universe.

According to Whitehead God should not be viewed as an exception to the categorical scheme. Hence he must be understood as prehending all other entities and being prehended by them. Prehension involves selective reenaction. Hence something of what is present in each moment of my experience is a reenaction of some element of the divine experience. God is causally efficacious in every experience; or in other words, in every moment everyone prehends God.

This prehension of God is never trivial. On the contrary, it is absolutely essential to and decisive for the becoming of each occasion. I mentioned that the principle of selection from the initial data is the subjective aim of the new occasion. Whitehead shows that this subjective aim must have also an initial phase and that this initial aim can only be understood as derived from God. Thus the fundamental purpose of self-realization around which each new moment of experience actualizes itself is a part of God's causal efficacy for it. Apart from this causal efficacy of God for the new occasion it could not occur at all.

The initial aim derived from God for each occasion is the ideal possibility for that occasion given the total situation. In its self-actualization the human occasion approximates that ideal only to some relative degree. For this failure to actualize in each moment the ideal possibility afforded us by God, we are, of course responsible, since the final self-determination of each occasion is its own.

Since every occasion receives its initial aim from God, the diversity in the relations with God in respect to this aim enjoyed by different persons lies in two factors. The first is the diversity of aims, and the second is the diverse degrees of approximation of the outcome to the ideal aim. For these reasons Whitehead's philosophy is open to the supposition that the aims provided by God for the successive occasions of Jesus' experience were markedly different from those provided by God for other persons. It is also open to the supposition of an identity or virtual identity of Jesus' self-actualization with the ideal aim, that does not appear elsewhere in history. Obviously, the factual judgment that Jesus was in these respects unique or even unusual cannot be made on philosophical grounds alone—only the judgment that such differences are possible.

This does not exhaust the ways in which the relation of God to Jesus may have been special. Although the philosophical scheme only requires that every occasion prehend God in some way, and its derivation of the initial aim might suffice, Whitehead believes that at least many occasions prehend God in other ways as well. Consider again the prehension by yourself in one moment of your immediately preceding experience. Part of what you prehend is the purpose that past had for this present, but in addition you prehend many other feelings and meanings as well. Furthermore, in some instances it may even be the purpose of the earlier occasion that it be fully felt in its successor.

In the same way God may be experienced by a human occasion in terms of other aspects of his divine experience besides his specific purpose for the becoming occasion. Furthermore, it may in some instances be the ideal aim for the new occasion that it prehend God in a peculiarly full and rich way. If this is the case, we may suppose that Jesus was unusual or unique in the way in which God willed to present himself to him and in the fullness with which in conforming himself to God's ideal aim for him, he received that presence.

If we understand "incarnation" in an Antiochene sense rather than in an Alexandrine one, I believe that Whitehead's conceptuality allows for an explication unmatched in Christian history. That is, if we assume the full personal humanity of Jesus, then the problem of understanding incarnation is the problem of understanding how God can be genuinely, personally present in one human individual in a way he is not present in all. Whitehead's doctrine of prehension as the one mode of real relation offers us an invaluable clue.

When I prehend in one moment of my experience the immediately preceding experience, I reenact that experience more or less fully. That means that that experience actually recurs in the new experience. It is *incarnate* there. This does not mean that the subjective immediacy of the past experience, its integrity as a unique individual entity, recurs. That would be impossible. Every experience is a single individual unrepeatable entity, and as *that* actuality it can never recur. But its qualitative character, its intentions and aims can and do recur, and recur as the contribution of that past entity. Indeed, each new occasion is constituted by the recurrence in it of that which has occurred in its past. Thus the past is *really* present, not only *to* but also *in* the present, giving to that present most of the richness and depth it enjoys.

One element in that reenacted or incarnated past, we have already seen, is God. But except for the unconscious derivation of the initial aim from him, most occasions of human experience reenact little if anything of the divine life. Perhaps any such reenaction is not in accordance with God's aim for them. But we may suppose a case in which God does aim to be the main content of that which is reenacted or incarnated from the past, so that an occasion of human experience would not so much reenact its own human past as some important aspect of the divine actuality. In such a case surely we could say with full literalness that God was incarnate in that human experience. If our historical evidence apprehended in faith warrants the claim that God was uniquely and decisively present *in* Jesus, Whitehead's philosophy enables us to understand the character of such a relationship.

Further, with this conceptuality we can see how God could be *in* Jesus on his own initiative without loss of the full personal freedom appropriate to Jesus' humanity. The initial aim is given by God, and only where God gives an initial aim that includes the primary effectiveness of the causal efficacy of his own experience can that experience have that efficacy. Jesus must be understood as selected for such a relation to God. On the other hand, the selection as a recurring act of God must in its turn be seen as dependent upon Jesus' response, and that response is not determined but only made possible by God's initiatory act.

Finally, the conceptuality of prehension allows us to avoid the common danger of supposing that if God is *in* Jesus, some aspect of Jesus' humanity must be thereby displaced. It is the essential character of an actual occasion of experience that its constituent elements are the presence *in* it of other entities. The presence in me of other entities does not violate my unique individuality and self-determination but rather makes that individuality and self-determination possible. There is no displacement, there is rather empowerment. Hence, if Jesus prehended God not only in his receiving of the initial aim but also in other and more unusual ways, that means a vast enrichment of the past out of which in each new moment Jesus' own unity of experience came to be formed. The presence of God in Jesus would mean incomparable increase in his personal freedom and humanity.

# III

Any adequate discussion of the finality of Jesus from a Whiteheadian perspective would not only have to develop the points made above much more fully but also introduce additional dimensions. In the first part of the chapter I argued that the kind of existence embodied in Jesus is historically final. Yet this in itself, even if it were successfully demonstrated, would leave many unanswered questions. These hinge especially on the relationship of the existence known by those who accept Jesus to Jesus' existence. There is, first, the question of the qualitative resemblance and difference of these modes of existence and, second, the question of the way in which the one gives rise to the other. In the second part of the chapter I argued that Whitehead enables us to understand the way in which God was present to and in Jesus. This gives rise to the question as to how God is present to and in the believer and further the question as to how the believer's relationship to God is related to his relationship to Jesus. The affirmation of the finality of Jesus normally involves the claim that through faith in him man enters into a final relationship also with God.

I believe that Whiteheadian conceptuality has rich possibilities for illuminating these questions in all their interconnections, but it is obviously impossible to carry out such a program in the space remaining in this chapter. I shall instead limit my remaining comments to one topic, involved in the foregoing questions but by no means exhausting them. That is the question of the relationship of the believer to Jesus. Of course, one part of this relationship is the believer's knowledge of Jesus' life and its impact on those who knew him. But for many Christians there has seemed to be some sense in which Jesus was present to them other than at this informational level. My thesis is that this sense of presence may not be altogether illusory.

Philosophically the issue hinges on the question of the causal efficacy of past events for the present or, in other words, the way in which a present occasion of experience prehends past occasions of experience. My belief is that Whitehead shows us the possibility of the unmediated prehension by a present entity of other entities in the past, even the distant past, and that the experience of some Christians seems to involve this kind of experience of Jesus. Because of the incredulity with which such an affirmation is likely to be met in our day, I will offer a brief suggestion as to the way in which it can be defended.

Once again we must consider the character of causality, but here with specific reference to time. This is a subject on which common sense and philosophy are alike profoundly confused. If you consider typical models for the understanding of causality you may conclude either that the cause is contemporary with the effect or that the cause is prior to the effect. If I take a rigid stick and push an object with it, the motion of the stick as cause seems to be contemporary with the motion of the object as effect. On the other hand, if I push a ball, the motion of the ball caused by my shove seems to come after the shove.

148

Positivistic philosophy since Hume has decided to solve the problem of cause by rejecting the category. We can describe either concomitant or successive changes and indicate statistical correlations between them. On this basis predictions can be made. There is nothing more to be said, for no additional relation between the changes can be observed.

Hume's critique of causality clearly shows that the fundamental notion underlying the term does not arise from sensory observation of environmental changes. Rather it arises in the immediacy of human experience itself. I find that the relation between the openness of my eyes and my visual experience gives itself to my experience as a causal one. I cannot but believe that certain events in the eye have a profound causal efficacy for my experience of color. Likewise I cannot but believe that my thoughts have a causal influence on my hand as I write these words. I experience my experience as both effect and cause of other events in my body. If I am told that this is a matter of statistical correlation only, I remain incredulous.

These causal relations between my eye and my experience and between my experience and the motion of my fingers involve temporal succession. We might not be able to recognize this introspectively, but physiologically it is well established. Messages are communicated through the nerves at a fantastic but finite speed. Cause precedes effect. This is further supported by the examples of causality I employed earlier where I spoke of the impact of one momentary human experience upon its successor. In this relationship, clearly, temporal succession exists between cause and effect.

If now we take the notion of causality as it arises in subjective personal experience and speculate that something like it obtains also among the real individual entities in the rest of nature, we find interesting and useful confirmation. According to the theory of relativity, the contemporary is defined precisely as the unrelated. All real physical relations obtain between the past and the present. The possibility of causal efficacy between contemporaries is excluded.

Thus far I have argued for one simple point that many would gladly have conceded, namely that causal relations always involve time and that the cause always precedes the effect. It has been necessary to elaborate the argument because the doctrine that the cause precedes the effect has far stranger consequences than we ordinarily recognize, and my further speculations hinge on the acceptance of these strange consequences.

If the cause is always in the past of the effect, this means that something that no longer exists, and indeed *only* something that no longer exists, has efficacy in the present. Common sense avoids the offense of this doctrine by assuming that although the entity that functions as cause has ceased to exist, it has only just *now* ceased to exist. One thinks of the impulse as beginning in the past but continuously moving into the future. As long as the idea of a continuum of motion is uppermost, the scandal of a causally efficacious past seems tolerable. However, we now know that neither in the nervous system nor in the subatomic world can the idea of continuous motion be employed. There are discrete occurrences that cease before they become effective for successors. The cause is *really* in the past of the effect as something finished and discrete.

If we genuinely recognize that all the causal influences on the present are past, then we must grant to the past some significant status. It is not enough, although certainly true, to state that the past is now nonexistent. It is a very peculiar type of nonexistence, namely, a causally efficacious nonexistence.

Once an entity has changed from the status of being presently existent to that of being nonexistent, there is no ontological necessity for supposing a further change from being a causally efficacious nonexistent to being a nonefficacious nonexistent.

If a past event of 1/10 second ago can exercise direct causal efficacy for me now, what of a past event of one second ago? Is there in principle any difference?

So long as we take our models for conceiving causal efficacy from billiard balls, whatever the philosophical possibilities, our instinctive answer is that the causal efficacy of the earlier event exhausted itself in its contribution to its immediate successor and is now only indirectly effective. But we have seen that at the level of billiard balls the concept of causality is at best misleading. If we turn instead to the fundamental basis of reflection on causality, our own immediate experience, and if we divorce ourselves from the prejudices derived from Newtonian mechanics, the answer seems to be quite different.

When, for example, a childhood experience vividly returns to consciousness with much of its emotive tone after years of being consciously wholly forgotten, how are we to understand what has happened? Are we to suppose that the full richness of that moment has been actually present in every intervening experience? This would require us to think of the unconscious as possessing a completeness of retention of every past experience that staggers the imagination and seems profoundly implausible. Or are we to think of the brain as having retained a physiological analogue of that experience utterly intact through all these years and then as suddenly releasing it. This attributes to the brain a kind of storage capacity that even its amazing complexity cannot begin to justify. What seems to occur is that the distant past experience itself is directly causally efficacious in the present experience.

I grant that the thought of immediate influence of a remote past event on the present is as baffling to our ordinary ways of thought as is the unchanged presence of that remote past in the unconscious or in the brain through all the intervening experiences. My argument, however, is that this strangeness is the

151

product of failure to recognize that *all* causal efficacy is of the now not-existing. Once this is really understood, the question of temporal proximity can be seen as a secondary one. Since our experience seems to give us numerous instances of the influence of past experiences other than the immediately preceding one on present experience, and since there is no ontological difficulty in affirming this kind of relation, I wish quite simply to assert its occurrence.

Now we must ask whether the only past experiences that can affect our present experience are those we identify as our own. In terms of the general Whiteheadian framework there is no reason to suppose that this would be the case, and Whitehead himself thought that there is empirical evidence that this is not the case. He refers to instances of mental telepathy as indicating the immediate influence of other persons' experiences upon us. I will not argue about this much-disputed matter except to say that I am personally convinced that the resistance to acceptance of the evidence in favor of mental telepathy arises from basic assumptions as to its impossibility rather than from any lack of empirical evidence. Since Whitehead's philosophy both allows the possibility and provides a thoroughly intelligible explanation of how it occurs, I am persuaded of its factuality.

Normally, mental telepathy seems to be the prehension by one experience of an immediately preceding experience of another person. Since we have seen that prehensions may occur of past experiences that are not temporally proximate, and since we are now affirming that there can be prehensions of experiences of other persons, we are finally prepared to ask whether the prehensions of the experiences of other persons must always be of immediately past experiences, or whether they too may be of the more remote past. Once again there is nothing in Whitehead's philosophy to preclude such prehensions of remote past experiences of other persons. Whether or not such prehensions occur is a purely factual question.

It cannot be denied that some persons report experiences that they understand as of this sort. Some sensitives seem to be able to describe experiences associated with the past history of objects presented to them. Occasionally persons have reported vivid experiences of the way a particular landscape appeared in past times. Claimed memories of previous lives could well be interpreted in these terms without resort to the hypothesis of transmigration. Some sense can be made of the depth psychological doctrine of a collective unconscious if we posit a direct unconscious prehension of innumerable experiences of the remote past.

I realize, of course, the great amount of incredulity that must be overcome before any of these phenomena or theories can gain serious attention in our day. That they have nevertheless continued to play some role in modern life and that students have been persuaded of the factuality of remarkable phenomena, whatever explanation is to be accorded them, suggests to me that human experience is far richer and more complex than ordinarily recognized. My conviction here again is that we should at least approach these phenomena with an open mind and that Whitehead's philosophy enables us to do so. When we do so, we gain some empirical support for the speculation that there are immediate prehensions of remote past experiences.

I assume that the vast majority of such prehensions are unconscious, and that most of these are trivial in their influence upon the present. On the other hand, some that are unconscious, may yet have important effects. Others may dimly qualify consciousness, and on very rare occasions some may even enter into vivid consciousness. If we continue our speculation as to how it happens that some of these past events have a significant direct influence on the present, we will do best to generalize from those less rare occasions on which an event in our own past suddenly becomes vividly present to us. This sometimes occurs without any apparent cause in the present. However, it is more often triggered by some aspect of the present situation. We speak of being reminded by something. Or we are guided by a skilled psychologist down a chain of associations, or under hypnosis a suggestion of the hypnotist is effective in causing us to reenact some part of our past.

This general discussion of the causal effect of the past upon the present is intended to set a context in which it becomes possible to take seriously the claim of some Christians that Jesus is immediately and effectively present in their lives. I am arguing that the unmediated prehension of past occasions even in the lives of others is possible. I would suggest that an attitude of expectancy, attention, and belief would be likely to facilitate such prehension and to determine which elements of the past should be prominent in their causal efficacy upon the present. Where such an attitude of expectancy, attention, and belief directed toward Jesus is shared with a community, as in the sacrament of the Lord's Supper, the possibility of the effective presence of Jesus to the individual believer is still further heightened. But the same presence might occur in private prayer, or even when there is no observable occasion for its occurence in the immediate situation.

In itself the presence of Jesus to the believer proves nothing about his finality. If a case is to be made for finality, it must be in terms of the consequences in our existence of his presence and especially the consequences for our relationship to God. For the Christian the relationship to Jesus is experienced as the one adequate ground for his relationship to God. That this is true can only be confessed, not argued.

# 7

## THE FINALITY OF CHRIST IN AN ESCHATOLOGICAL PERSPECTIVE

The affirmation of the finality of Christ is at best a theological option. However, it is a dubious option. For truth is an attribute of its occurrence, and Christ's finality does not occur when Christ is being affirmed as final. The history of Christology is the graveyard for just such direct claims about Jesus of Nazareth, because direct claims have no essential capacity to evoke a living faith. Jesus was believed to be anointed by God for the fulfillment of a mission. Yet the history of theology has been the history of the adulation of his person, and grandiose claims for Christ have lacked an essential connection with "what really happened." The titles of Jesus express a quite different reality when considered as events of disclosure than when considered as predicates of Jesus' person.

The first important break with Christology as direct claim for Christ came in the Protestant Reformation, when theology replaced what had become honorific personal titles with titles which indicated what he really did, titles bearing upon his functions, his offices, generally called the offices of prophet, priest, and king. The second and even more decisive break with the history of Christology has occurred in modern times in the realization that the person of Jesus functioned within an entirely echatological horizon. Because of that, it can now be seen that finality is not an attribute of Jesus of Nazareth himself, in his person, but of the eschaton whose imminence he signalizes. Finality as a christological claim, then, is not a wholly salutary option. The finality of Christ in the horizon of eschatology, however, is not optional at all, but simply redundant.

The primacy of eschatology in Christian understanding has come to light quite recently as a consequence of modern man's ability to treat the sources of faith with historical seriousness. Biblical exegetes applying modern historiography have come to know the nature of the early faith better than the apostles knew it themselves, and differently than the dogmaticians, who until now have expanded upon and embroidered around the apparent historical gaps in the apostolic faith. Despite the great range of emphasis in current interpretations of eschatology, Jesus of Nazareth is unanimously regarded as an eschatological reality. The implication in that consensus is that it is unwise for the church to continue to build its faith upon claims for the person of Christ in himself.

Christology in the horizon of eschatology is nevertheless an important factor in eschatology. For one thing, a proper Christology has kept the church from allowing its eschatological message to become engulfed by apocalypticism. Apocalypticism is both ahistorical and anthropocentric. It is ahistorical because of the way it depreciates the world in the interests of an otherworldly future. Eschatology, on the other hand, ties the thought of God to the reality of history. Apocalypticism is anthropocentric, because apocalyptic "last things" visualize Christ as the judge of man according to human merits. The eschatology of the New Testament, however, is a fundamentally christological reality, tutoring man in the expectation of what God has brought about in Christ, rather than of what pious men will deserve. Apocalypticism may well have been the dominant theology of the early church, and, as such, set Christology off on the wrong foot, making claims for Christ based on his alleged possibilities for the future, rather than on the achieved realities of his mission. The expectation of the kingdom of God in the preaching of Jesus, on the other hand, had the power to transform the world through the response of repentance. When his death and resurrection appeared to have terminated his preaching, direct claims for Christ were allowed to supplant his indirect, kerygmatic effect. When these claims were apocalyptic, they converted faith, which was a bona fide transformation of history, into an attitude of waiting. The person of Jesus illuminated by his achieved history, however, serves as an open rebuke to the ahistorical and anthropocentric deviations of apocalypticism.

Christology is a significant aspect of eschatology for another reason. It now seems plausible, from a historical vantage point upon the early faith, that soteriology became the church's alternative to its ailing apocalyptic. Christological gains were made in the early ecumenical councils on the basis of soteriological alternatives to apocalypticism. In order to forgive sins, it was argued, Christ must have been more than a man, hence the direct claims for his deity. Eschatology, however, when seen as the horizon within which christological statements are to be made, subordinates soteriology, with its emphasis on Jesus' role in the forgiveness of sins, to history, with its call for a change of orientation toward the world. Forgiveness of sins is a phenomenon known prior to and outside the Christian movement, hence not at all unique to it. When it is taken up into Christianity, it is simply instrumental to eschatology. If Jesus himself underwent no transition from sin to salvation, why should such a motif be thought so central to the faith which he inaugurates? If Jesus in his associations and in his preaching accepted sinners on God's behalf, why should it be

157

thought necessary to floriate his chaste preaching into baroque myths of sacrifice based upon his cross? But forgiveness of sins is announced by Jesus in order to free men for the new age of responsibility for the world, as defined by the imminence of God and his kingdom. The history of theology has acknowledged the purely prefatory character of forgiveness wherever holiness and not forgiveness has been the distinctive mark of faith.[1] To have turned Christ into a new agent of salvation, replete with the soteriological claims which Judaism had applied to its altars and Hellenism to its cults, was to have blunted the edge of his mission to make God's reign imminent through preaching.

Therefore, the finality of Christ from an eschatological point of view is the finality of the eschaton whose imminence he heralds. In the event of his inauguration of God's kingdom, *Christ fulfills the office of prophet.* He is prophet, but not because he points to some far-off event in which God will yet manifest himself. He is prophet in such a way as to put an end to prophecy. In his word all that God promises is realized. (Luke 4:21.) The God of the future is brought into the present. Hope is grounded in faith. Standing with him in his word, men now have faith, which is the final mode both of their being with God and of their being in the world. *Christ also fulfills the office of priest.* He is priest, not primarily because he intercedes for us at the right hand of the father, but because he puts an end to the law, which is the occasion for sin because it tempts men to live without trust. Thus he strikes a blow at the institution of priesthood which exists for the mediation of forgiveness. Now that the eschaton has ended the age of law, men no longer need to exploit the world for religious purposes, using it as the

[1] See my essay, "The Hermeneutics of Holiness in Wesley," in *The Heritage of Christian Thought,* Robert E. Cushman and Robert Lowry Calhoun, eds. (New York: Harper & Row, 1965), pp. 127-41.

arena for fulfillment of the law and thus for self-vindication. All such piety is terminated when Jesus of Nazareth on God's behalf accepts sinners notwithstanding the condemnation of the law. *Christ also fulfills the office of king.* Not that in so doing he reduces man to the status of servant, lordship being unique only to him. He rather redefines lordship in terms of servanthood. From now on it is the last who shall be first. Then he passes the royal status on to man, a status distinguished by the crown of thorns, hallmark of the eschaton. By his words and acts, then, in one event Jesus united men with God in the purposes of his kingdom, overcoming their religious bondage to the world which the law enforced and setting them free for responsible stewardship in the world. Understood in that way, the definition of Christ in the Chalcedonian formula is essentially eschatological. The Chalcedonian formula in calling Christ "truly man and truly God, without separation and without confusion" gives testimony to the finality of Christ because it means that God's destiny for man is immutably tied to what Jesus of Nazareth has done. Thus Christology is primarily eschatology and the finality of Christ is a truth occurring within the horizon of eschatology.

At least three large problems confront us in these generalizations. What do they mean? How can we believe them? Why do they signify finality?

# I

Eschatology means that in some sense Christ is the "end of the world." But what is meant by "end" and by "world"? "End" does not connote a limitation in some spatial or temporal sense, but a determination. One does not "expect" an eschaton as one expects the end of a journey or the end of an affair. Eschaton is an end insofar as one lives under its influence. Nor does "end" connote a cessation, such as death imposes upon life, but a coming to fulfillment. The fulfillment involved, however, may not be simply by anticipation, as of some larger realization yet to come. Eschatology does not have to do with what will be the case when history has run its course, known now only in part. Eschatology is the knowledge that the sort of reality which comes to expression because of Christ is reality in its final form and that this reality is all-we-have-and-all-we-need to go by. Paul, for instance, may not really be complaining when he says, "Now we see through a glass darkly," as if counseling the Corinthians to await some face-to-face encounter. He is inviting the church to the resolve of faith which is in itself the eschatological existence, an existence in which it is *better* to believe *not* having seen. Or, again, the words of John's Gospel on Jesus' lips, "until I come," are the words of primitive Christian apocalyptic. Therefore, they are not normative for faith and are immediately challenged in the very next verse, which safely lodges the answer to the question of Christ's return in Christ's own secret will. (John 21:22, 23.) Therefore, when Jesus says to his disciples in his farewell address, "yet a little while and I will come to you," he is not endorsing apocalypticism, because, in fact, he immediately advises them that the world will see him no more. For the New Testament faith the judgment of the world is fulfilled in Christ. To know that Christ will be with us always is, therefore, to enter "a new history" [2] which will end all other histories and bring all other worlds under judgment by its finality.

When one says of eschatology that it designates the "end of the *world*," one means by "world" a fundamentally historical reality. For that reason the early church's attitude toward

[2] Rudolf Bultmann, *Das Evangelium des Johannes* (16th ed.; Göttingen: Vandenhoeck and Reprecht, 1959), p. 476.

apocalypticism was justifiably ambivalent. Apocalypticism was a development in late Judaism which visualized a universalism for God's relation to the world is a geographical and ethnic extensiveness unprecedented in earlier Hebrew thinking. God's apocalypse would be a revelation, not simply to Israel, but, so to say, to the "world." At the same time, the apocalypse was to occur through cosmographic manifestations which gave to "world" the connotation more of what we now know as nature, than as history. But when it comes to the world cosmologically conceived, eschatology is closer to the prophetic than to the apocalyptic tradition. While apocalypticism visualized a radically new world, it did so in terms more expressive of worlds of nature than of worlds of history. While prophetism visualized changes being made within the present world form, it expressed these changes in largely historical terms. When the New Testament does seem to be expressing its eschatology in the cosmological terms of apocalyptic, those expressions are usually in the service rather of the history of salvation. To take a single example, when the letter to the Ephesians holds up hope for the ultimate reconciliation of the "cosmos," it is clearly referring to the uniting of Jews and Gentiles in "one body," the church (2:11-22), a historical entity.

"World" in the New Testament, then, is not a quasi-scientific construct, a cosmographic arena upon which history plays out its game. World is a dominantly historical reality, a matrix of relationships into which, when one is fitted, one derives the meaning of one's own existence. Yet, world is not a space which preexists one's participation in it. It is the relationship which comes to fulfillment as one has his being-in it. World is not the box one is in. World is the mode of one's being-in. Thus there is the scientific world, the sports world, the art world. Yet, like the horizon, a world is not the creature or the product of man but rather makes the discoverability of man a possibility. For

161

"world" is the kind of reality which has a fundamental expressibility—in acts, gestures, and words. The end of the "world" to which eschatology refers is the end of the world which occurs when through his symbolic action and his parabolic speech, Jesus of Nazareth exposes the life of man to the horizon of God's imminent kingdom, giving man a whole new mode of being-in.

Interpreters seem clear that eschatology does not involve a timeless truth. The reason usually given is that it is a truth which happens and therefore is eventful. That, however, is not the full story. Eschatology is a truth which occurs under the conditions of time, which is not mere eventfulness, but transience and finitude. Are not the expectations in finality and finitude incompatible? In apocalyptic, yes. In eschatology, no. The decision between eschatology and apocalyptic was made once and for all by Jesus of Nazareth in the Garden of Gethsemane in his final hours when he refused to ask God to rescue him from death. That eschaton is the horizon which continues to bring man's very finitude to light as final. Eternal life is not deliverance from finitude but obedience to God even unto death and the realization that God can be glorified by an obedient death. (John 12:27, 28.)

Those who understand the temporality of the eschaton do not always realize that they must also choose against its universality. Universality may be possible in a theology of grace where God's acts prevail despite their actualization in life. Or, universality may be possible in a cosmological theology where God's acts have relevance for things apart from mediation by men. But the eschatological world is a world of rapture over the joy of faith, and faith, unlike grace, is man's life qualified consciously by the presence of God in the person of Jesus of Nazareth. The joyful world of the eschaton is the world of a happiness which *knows* it is happy. As John Wesley once put it, "No man can be justified and not know it!" [3]

Under the parabolic proclamation of Jesus, the truth of the eschaton is a historical truth. That means that the truth does not inhere in the correspondence of propositions with the things they signify. Parabolic propositions are not words which signify things. The words are the things. Luther knew that when he understood that the justification which comes by faith alone is also by word alone. Wesley knew it when he referred to the redeeming blood of Christ as "a speaking blood." [4] Parabolic truth inheres in the events in which words bring to expression a new world, a new history, a newly qualified consciousness. If such events are final, as the term "eschaton" implies they are, they will have to be final, then, in a sense that includes neither infinite nor universal. And if such events are of the character of worlds, then they are worlds which live by words, worlds like creation itself, if, indeed, God created the world by his word. One could therefore say that Jesus of Nazareth has talked the world into the kingdom of God, or, more accurately, Jesus has talked the kingdom of heaven down to earth. Little wonder, then, that the gospel of John has called him "the word," the apostle Paul has interpreted faith as an acoustical affair, and the Synoptic Gospels record that he said nothing to the people without a parable. (Matt. 13:34.)

## II

How does one arrive at such a vast conclusion about the eschatological significance of Jesus of Nazareth? In the same

[3] "Minutes of Some Late Conversations," I, Question 5. *The Works of John Wesley*, authorized edition of 1872, VIII (Grand Rapids, Mich.: Zondervan Publishing House, 1959), 276.

[4] Sermon XVI, i, 12.

way Jesus did—historically; therefore, in the same way one would arrive at anything historical. Jesus of Nazareth, a fully historical being, was placed in a world. Worlds are invitations to decipher meaning and to reshape the world by that newly deciphered meaning. Worlds are historical realities. A world is a structure of reality in which tradition and interrogation interact in a circular way. Questions interrogate events and events illuminate questions. In the process of the historical world meanings sedimented in historical events are stirred up by mankind's sentiment for meaning. "Are you he who is to come?" "Whom do men say that I am?" The circular dialogue between traditional meanings and the quest for meaning is only terminated by a risk of judgment, such as, "thy will be done!"

As historical beings, men stand within events which are conferring meaning. Jesus is no exception to this fundamentally historical structure. He is the one through whom it comes to evidence in history that the God of the future has come into the present as the basis for man's ongoing life. In his baptism he is brought to light as the Messiah and the kingdom of God dawns. (John 1:26, 31.) His baptism, therefore, is the sacrament of eschatological history. In his parables he is speaking as one who is already standing within the eschatological nearness of God. (Luke 4:21.) Like a poet who always says more than he knows, Jesus in his parables brings to expression the movement of God's kingdom. His expression provides the basis for his comprehension of himself and bursts like lightning over the terrain of his whole time. He says, "The kingdom of God is like . . ." and the world is swept up into the kingdom. He says, "I am," and the world articulates back to him its newfound stance, "Thou art!" In his preaching Jesus stands as the sign of the kingdom of God that is upon him and in whose presence there is no neutrality.

164

But that was in his time. How does our time any longer sense the imminence of God's kingdom? The answer is: We do it in the same way Jesus did, except that now we do it within his horizon. His eventfulness is sedimented in the history into which we now direct our sentiment for meaning. We make the risk of judgment that he made, but on the basis of his judgment. To be a man of faith is to live in remembrance of him. Our resolve will decide whether his judgment will find its consummation in our history. Luther alleged this to be Paul's meaning when he said in Galatians, "The life I live is Christ." Christ is *mea forma*. That means that the eschaton comes in the speaking of Jesus and continues to come when the church remembers Jesus in its speaking, that is, when the church enters into the horizon of understanding within which Jesus stood when he spoke.

In Richard Kim's novel, *The Martyred*, the son of a Korean minister has revolted against his father's faith and has become a professor of history in the University. The father, I believe, is justifiably confident in his son's spiritual destiny, not because as a Presbyterian he is convinced that in the end God will unite all things in himself. Rather, as he said, "If one is a good historian . . . he will invariably come to the large question of whether or not history must have an end one day. . . . If he does that some day, then I shall have to admit that we are not so far apart from each other as it might appear." Kim said that what the pastor had in mind was not "some sort of teleological question. . . . No, he said, it was an eschatological question." [5]

Christian faith is a fundamentally historical enterprise, not despite its eschatology but because of it. Jesus of Nazareth brought a new horizon to bear upon history. Because the church

[5] (New York: George Braziller, 1964), p. 168.

reminds us of his word, his horizon still mobilizes us, so long, that is, as it answers to something in us, to our sentiment for meaning. We must not assume that we are being historical if we think of his words in detachment from our own concerns, any more than we are being historical if we attempt to conserve the laws of the land as they were at their inception. When Jesus said to Nicodemus, "Ye must be born again," he was not issuing a universal command. He was sensitizing Nicodemus' preunderstanding.[6] To acknowledge the importance of a pre-understanding is to concede that the meaning at stake in any relationship is something that will occur in one's own situation. We now bring that prior question to our faith as the faith has been traditioned by its history: Is there anything in the words of Jesus heard across these centuries by which we may be "born again," anything which promises us something we still really want? If there is not, then we shroud the church in the shawl of a sect, standing guard over claims we are able to venerate, but which no longer give birth to a history for us, claims we can express in our will to rhetoric, but which no longer quicken our imaginations. Theologians who are resisting this sectarian trend for the sake of a lively historical meaning ought not be written off as innovators whose passions (as Eusebius of Caesarea once warned) only lead to heresy. An irrevocable conviction which does not move the world is no fitting symbol for a faith whose lord defined his existence as mission.

Two such convictions especially thwart the birth of faith in our time. One is no serious temptation to Methodists. It is a futuristic eschatology which sees in the doctrine of the resurrection of the dead "the absolute metaphor." [7] All other meta-

[6] Bultmann, Das Evangelium des Johannes, p. 106.

[7] Wolfhart Pannenberg, Grundzüge der Christologie (Gütersloh, 1964), Blumenberg's phrase, p. 189, used approvingly by Pannenberg.

phors in Christian preaching are taken to be merely proleptic moments of that metaphor, such as Jesus' resurrection, but conceivably also the life-giving word of Jesus in his parabolic metaphors. The warrant for this view is that it is strong in the early church and can even be said to have been the dominant theology of the early church. Its objectionable feature is not simply that it becomes a species of eschatological verification for Christian faith, delaying the real engagement with the world to some far-off divine event. The real objection is to the way it depreciates the eschatological significance of Jesus' historical eventfulness. There is a theology implicit in the preaching of Jesus which conflicts with the allegedly dominant apocalyptic theology of the early church. The new quest for the historical Jesus has brought it more clearly to light than previously in the church. The meaning of that message is that the eschaton comes, not in the chronological last days of history, but in the speech of Jesus. Jesus' resurrection is a sign, as the gospel of John makes clear. But it is a sign, not of his future conquests, but of the victory already achieved in his word, of which he says, "I have overcome the world" (John 16:33). Faith looks for nothing more. Apocalyptic theology awaited God in the distance. New Testament eschatology brought the distant God near. We ought not be allowed to forget that the characteristic literary form of early Christianity was not the apocalypse, but the gospel.[8]

The other conviction which may thwart a candid arrival of faith is more peculiarly Methodist, even though it existed in the early church as a major alternative to futuristic eschatologies. It is the doctrine of the Holy Spirit in so far as the Holy Spirit is said to be our continuity with Christ. An understanding of

---

[8] Gerhard Ebeling, "Der Grund Christlicher Theologie," *Zeitschrift für Theologie und Kirche*, LVIII (August, 1961), 232.

history and language has made that use of the doctrine superfluous as it was superfluous in certain sectors of the early
church. The distinction made between human witness and the
witness of the Holy Spirit is a distinction familiar, for instance,
to the Acts of the Apostles, but not to the Gospel of John,
not even to the Synoptic Gospels. Mark, for instance, has no
narrative regarding the post-Easter descent of the Spirit upon
the disciples. For the Gospel of John the paraclete who will
relieve Jesus, as in the changing of the guard, is the word of
preaching. Witness to the word is not a second reality alongside the witness of the spirit. Why is it not the case, then,
that the word for us as for Jesus is the mode in which God
makes himself present? Those who hear the preaching of the
church hear Jesus, not because some independent action of
the Holy Spirit makes him present, but because the word itself
overcomes chronological distance. Those who hear Jesus hear
the Father, not because the Holy Spirit intercedes, but because
the human word itself has the power in history to substitute
for God. The doctrine of the Holy Spirit in this relation becomes a mythological way of alluding to "the power of preaching in the church." The intention of the myth was utterly
kerygmatic. It means to conserve the valid and indispensable
conviction that when the word is preached it is God's word
that is heard, word in the dimension of eschatological disclosure.
The church's historiographical responsibility in exegeting and
traditioning the apostolic faith has, however, often been weak-
ened by the myth of the Holy Spirit. Dependence on it also
fosters hopes for spiritual manifestations more powerful than
the plain meanings conveyed in merely human words. "Holy
Spirit" has been the church's way of saying "the presence of
God." Since Christ, however, the presence of God is given in
the word of Christ. It is true that in the first five centuries of
Christendom the doctrine of the Holy Spirit, taken up into

168

the formulation of the doctrine of the Trinity, was in effect a demythologizing of the polytheistic tendencies in the developing Christian doctrine of God. When the works of God in creation, revelation, and redemption began to splinter God three ways, to the jeopardy of monotheism, the church found a way of saying that Father, Son, and Holy Spirit are not three gods, but one God three times. It was also true, however, that the doctrine of the Holy Spirit in the early church was a rival to Jesus' eschatological message, even while being an alternative to apocalypticism.

## III

What of finality, then, is really brought to light when the word of Christ is spoken into our situation today? What does it mean to say that the word spoken by Jesus of Nazareth and heard by us today *is* the eschaton? If an eschatological event is an event in which faith is made possible, what is that structure which makes it so final?

To say this event is *unique* would not exhaust the meaning of its finality. In history all events are in some sense unique. To say it is *ultimate* would not be enough, either, because all events which occur through obedience to God are, in respect of their God-relation, ultimate. One question remains: What makes the Christ event *final*? What is there about Jesus of Nazareth that makes him absolutely important and valid for all the future? Why must salvation be bound up entirely with faith in him, so that the relation to him can be called the determination of the final destiny of men? Why is it legitimate to call him *alpha* and *omega* without any sense of doxological hyperbole? What can it mean to say that faith in God is so irrevocably dependent upon Jesus of Nazareth that the wisdom communicated in this event makes all other wisdom anachro-

nistic and obsolete, so that subsequent to this event nothing
can appear that will supersede it, indeed, so that man needs
to look nowhere else for God and God needs to do nothing
more, and so that Jesus can be said to have had the last word?

The question of the finality of Jesus is the question of what
it means that he has spoken of God. The revelatory significance
of Jesus' speech is not that he communicated information about
God, but that he stood in an event in which men were once
and for all enabled to let God be, even when they could
not say what he is. The eschatological encounter with God is
an encounter with a reality who allows himself to be brought
out of the future into the present. But it is not an apocalyptic
encounter, as with a child at hide-and-seek who, unfound, must
at last show himself. Jesus speaks of God in such a way as to
encounter men with God's hidden presence. Like a faithful
Jew who would rather call upon the kingdom of heaven than
upon the kingdom of God, he scarcely even uses the name of
God. One could almost say of him what Montaigne once said
of the apostle Paul: "Of all the cults St. Paul found in Athens,
the most pardonable of all seemed to him the one dedicated
to the 'unknown God.' " [9] Jesus' name for God is *ho pempsas
me*, "He that hath sent me" (John 1:33; 4:34; etc.). That is
why Christology is so crucial to theology: the identity of God is
somehow bound up with Jesus. And who, indeed, is Jesus? He
is "son of God" whose office is eschatological, namely, to finish
the Father's work. And what was the Father's work? To let
himself be revealed as "Father." Henceforth, anyone who has
seen Christ has seen the Father. Anyone who has received
Christ has received the Father. Anyone who has heard Christ
has heard the Father. Christ and the Father are one in an event

[9] *The Autobiography of Michel de Montaigne* (New York: Vintage
Books, 1956), p. 206.

of speech. If Philip's request is any solid indication of the human preunderstanding, Jesus' revelation of the Father is final: "Show us the Father," Philip asked, "and we shall be satisfied." When that revelation occurs, man's joy is said to be full, and no one can take it from him. (John 14:8, 15:11.)

The answer to the question of the finality of Jesus is not primarily that God is now known to be Father, but the historical effect of that realization, namely, that men understand themselves as sons of God. The eschaton, therefore, derives its finality, not so much from supernatural inferences about the presence of the Almighty as it does from the status conferred on history by the knowledge of man's sonship and the consequent insinuations of maturity in history.

The work of the Father which Jesus finished was to make men sons of God, no longer slaves or even children, but sons, and if sons, then heirs. Unlike a slave or a child, a son is an heir to whom the Father turns over responsibility for what is his. In the word of Jesus of Nazareth men are brought to maturity in the world by receiving the world as an inheritance from God which henceforth remains their responsibility. (Gal. 4 and Rom. 8.) The time in which that act occurs is the fullness of time. Thereafter man is to govern himself as one mature and not as those who are unstable in all their ways. (James 1:4 ff.) They are the mature, as contrasted with the babes. (Heb. 5:13.) In Christ men have been brought to completion. (Col. 2:10 NEB.) Precisely in the word in which God is addressed as Father, Jesus takes sonship upon himself and on God's behalf confers sonship upon those who hear his word. By that performatory word he turns the world over to men as their responsibility, and the ground of the world's maturity is once for all established. To hear the word "Father" addressed to God is to participate in an event in which man's sonship comes to expression.

171

Becoming a son (John 3:1-8) is being born into an eschatological existence, being set within a whole new history. To know oneself as son of God is not to have *information* about oneself. That would turn theology into anthropology. To know oneself as son is to receive the gift of humanity, that is, to have permission to be a man, that is, to be free to be only a man. In this event in which the Fatherhood of God becomes the basis for man's sonship, history emerges in its eschatological form. There one is free—free from all requirement for realizing salvation through the world, free from the fear of finding devils in the world, free from the possibility of identifying God with any part of the world, free from the psychological need to hide one's moral fears and failures from the world, free from the superstitutious ruse of using God to explain the wonders of the world, free from the fear of death because our life is lived toward God and not toward our own erosive future, free from any necessity to fill the future with conjectures based on our limited knowledge of the world, free from the temptation to derive our ultimate meaning from our limited tasks in the world, free from the problems which come in regarding the world as a riddle for men to solve, thus free from worldly care as are the birds of the air and the lilies of the field, free from what Aristotle called "the itch of desire," free like art, that is, which does not always have to be for-the-sake-of something, but can be simply what it is, as D. H. Lawrence said, "not bent on grabbing, because we know we inherit."

Jesus is final, then, because in him the conditions for immaturity in history have been terminated and the conditions for maturity are now at hand. Now we know what creation is. Creation is the matrix of relationships in which, because there is a God who is known as Father, men do not belong to the world but the world belongs to men. Creation is the historical structure of reality in which, because men receive the world from God, they can be responsible for it, not being responsible to it, not turning the creature into a creator and worshiping the creature, thus not forfeiting the grounds of responsibility for the creature.

Does it not seem in such an understanding of eschatology that God has abdicated and is virtually even dead, having nothing left to do? It is true that he has nothing left to do, except what he has already done, namely, to turn the world over to men, making them sons. But as Father, he remains the living ground for man's continuing sonship, thus for man's everlasting responsibility. When sons forfeit their inheritance, the Father does not reduce them again to servanthood, he reaffirms them in their sonship by giving the world back to them again, as the father did the prodigal. (Luke 15:11-32.) Therefore, we do not say with William Blake,

> Thou art a man, God is no more,
> Thy own humanity learn to adore.

The eschatological speech of Jesus remembered and renewed in the church liberates the creature from the self-preoccupation which perverts creaturehood into demonic bondage to the world. In Christ God delivers up his rule to men, but he continues to reign.

However, neither would we say in Thomas DeQuincey's rather eschatological terms (to use the paraphrase of J. Hillis Miller[10]), "In God's time all time is fulfilled, and the dreadful hemorrhage of time has stopped." Eschatology holds out no dilated hopes for man. It discloses the situation of man as it most really is. The eschaton is not that than which a greater cannot be thought, the dream of some humanly desirable

[10] The Disappearance of God (Cambridge: Harvard University Press, 1963), p. 73.

utopia. The eschaton is that than which a greater need no longer be sought now that the revelation of the end is at hand. Expressed in the lordship of Christ and his crown of thorns, eschatology sees obedience unto death as the "red badge of courage" in which the mature son is the one who willingly sheds his own blood in imitation of the obedience of Christ, not asking for more. The sower sows the seed. The rest is up to the land. (Mark 4:3-9.)

You may say to me, then "You allege as Christian what any modern man can know without that faith." I do not wholly deny it. Modern man has learned to get along without God in all the important affairs of his life, assuming a fully historical existence which is an existence in which man holds himself responsible for the world. I could, of course, attempt to register as a matter of history that modern men have not, in fact, known responsibility for the world without Christian faith. The eschaton is a *historical* reality. Why, then, should it seem strange that its effects are manifest even where its sources are unacknowledged? But I would rather say, in a less defensive vein, that devotees of Christian faith do not deplore modern man's apparently independent courage and responsibility. For Christians are not bent upon converting men to Christ. That evangelistic drive is abandoned with the abandonment of direct Christology and with the dawn of the eschatological horizon. Christians are responsible for announcing the eschaton and thus for bringing the world to expression as creation, as responsible sonship. Therefore, when we hold out faith to men, we do not do so in the expectation of taking something from them, or even of giving something to them which they do not have. We do so to confirm and strengthen them in what they could indeed already in some sense have. So may their sonship be brought out of latency and fate into patency and history, and their joy become final by being made full.

# 8

## THE FINISHED WORK OF CHRIST
## IN WORD AND SACRAMENT

Brueghel's astonishing picture of the Crucifixion might be taken at first sight for a cynical comment on its irrelevance. Hundreds of people are milling around, all occupied with their own affairs, and no single one of them so much as glances at the man who has stumbled under his cross. Only when one looks closely does he see that he is at the exact center of it all, that in him all the lines of the picture focus and cohere. History has vastly extended the frame to take in countless millions of other human beings, for the most part also unregarding, yet this immense claim stands. Here is a final, universal deed. And the work of Christ is bound up with his person. Long ago, it was the conviction sustaining Athanasius that only one who was truly God could save a world.

When the *Report on the Conversations Between the Church of England and the Methodist Church* appeared, it came under heavy fire from a group of Anglicans known as "conservative evangelicals." One of them, the Rev. R. T. Beckwith, has returned to the attack in a volume *Priesthood and Sacraments*.[1] Mr. Beckwith regards the section of the Report on the Sacraments as a sell-out by the Methodists to the Anglo-Catholics.

---

[1] (Appleford, Abingdon, Berkshire: The Marcham Manor Press, 1964).

He attributes the presence of the word "re-present" in that section to me. His evidence is the fact that in an essay on "Holy Communion" (1947) I rendered "anamnesis," by "re-present," and that this is the word used by Dom Gregory Dix in his famous *Shape of the Liturgy.* I must say, however, that I had nothing whatever to do with the appearance of the word in the Methodist Report. Moreover, Mr. Beckwith admits that this word "re-present" was used in this connection by the late Dr. A. W. Harrison as long ago as 1935.

I intrude this domestic affair upon this ecumenical audience because it is a peg to hang some important considerations upon, and, further, because at one point it concerns world Methodism. For Mr. Beckwith suggests that until we have purged ourselves of his suspicions, we should stop singing the sacramental hymns of Charles Wesley. Since as a world church we stopped this long ago, it is worth drawing attention to those hymns, and asking whether, in fact, John and Charles Wesley still believe and preach our doctrines.

Let us begin, then, with what the Report says about this word "re-present," that "The background of the Eucharist is the sacrifice of Christ, and Christ alone, on the Cross. It is that we represent and re-present and renew by our remembrance and communion." [2]

In his *Shape of the Liturgy* Dom Gregory Dix used the word "re-present" to distinguish the eucharistic memorial from a simple mental recollection of something past and absent. He did not use it in the sense of "offer again," but "In the Scriptures both of the Old and New Testament [it has] the sense of re-calling and re-presenting before God an event in the past, so that it becomes here and now operative by its effects. . . .

[2] (London: Church Information Office and The Epworth Press, 1963), p. 32.

[This is how] the eucharist is regarded both by the New Testament and by second century writers as the anamnesis of the passion." [3]

Anamnesis, then, implies something more than when an English schoolboy remembers the Battle of Hastings, or when the Daughters of the American Revolution remember Valley Forge. This distinction is, however, not some Anglo-Catholic idiosyncrasy. It is supported by impressive evidence on a wide spectrum.[4]

But altogether apart from theology, the distinction between two kinds of remembering, between mental recollection and the living evocation of the past by some sight or touch or action, is a familiar human experience. Marcel Proust in his "Recherche du temps perdu" tells how a bun dipped in a cup of tea may bring back in a moment a vanished childhood, and he says:

Information about the past which deliberate memory can convey preserves nothing of its true essence . . . but in this way a whole childhood swims into consciousness, not in the form of a series of intellectual recollections emptied of all power, but solid, alive, and still charged with the emotions. In that single moment time is regained, one whole section of the past has managed to become a section of the present.[5]

[3] (London: Dacre Press, 1947), p. 161.
[4] Gerhard Kittel, Theologisches Wörterbuch zum neuen Testament (Stuttgart: W. Kohlhammer, 1933), article by Johannes Behm, p. 351; Geoffrey Lampe, Lexicon of Patristic Greek (London: Oxford University Press, 1961), fasc. 1, "Anamnesis"; N. A. Dahl, "Anamnesis," Studia Theologica, I (Lund: C. W. K. Gleerup, 1947), pp. 70-85; J. D. Benoit, Liturgical Renewal (London: SCM Press, 1958), p. 44; M. Thurian, Eucharistic Memorial, 2 vols. (London: Lutterworth Press, 1963); N. Hook, Eucharist in the New Testament, (London: The Epworth Press, 1964). For argument on the other side see W. M. F. Scott in Theology, April and June, 1953.
[5] A. Maurois, The Quest for Marcel Proust (Mystic, Conn.: Laurence Verry, 1950), pp. 175-76.

And when we turn to corporate recollection, there is some interesting Old Testament study to support the distinction. Not to press Mowinckel and Pedersen,[6] there is a luminous monograph by B. S. Childs, *Memory and Tradition of Israel*. He says:

> The worshipper experiences an identification with the original events. He bridges the gap of historical time and participates in the original history. . . .
> The Biblical events can never become static, lifeless beads which can be strung on a chronological chain, the redemptive events of Israel's history do not come to rest, but continue to meet, and are contemporary with each generation.[7]

This renewal of the past in the present is not only important for the primitive Eucharist. Interesting studies in baptism by Rudolf Schnackenburg[8] and George Every[9] make the same point about the death-resurrection event. And it is true of the apostolic preaching. Dahl quotes a saying that it is true of the proclamation not of a sacred past but of a sacred present.[10] About this there is a famous passage by C. H. Dodd which is quoted by Dix and by the Methodist Report. Dodd borrows from C. C. J. Webb the idea of "corporate memory" and says, "In the eucharist the church perpetually constitutes the crisis in which the Kingdom of God came in history. . . . In the eucharist we are there—in the night in which he was betrayed,

[6] J. P. E. Pedersen, *Israel*, I (London: Oxford University Press, 1953), 256 ff.

[7] (Naperville, Ill.: Alec R. Allenson, 1962), pp. 82-83.

[8] *Baptism in the Thought of St. Paul* (Oxford: Blackwell and Mott, 1964).

[9] *The Baptismal Sacrifice* (London: SCM Press, 1959).

[10] "Amamnesis," p. 92, n. 1.

at Golgotha, before the empty tomb, . . . and at the moment of his coming, at the Last Trump." [11]

Mr. Beckwith scoffs at the idea of a corporate memory which includes the future. Yet is there not in this a hint of the New Testament reversal of time (Rom. 13:11-12)? Newman's profound sentences, a hundred years and more old, are curiously modern:

and hence, though time intervene between Christ's first and second coming, it is not *recognized* (as I may say) in the gospel scheme, but is, as it were, an accident. For so it was, that up to Christ's coming in the flesh, the course of things ran straight towards that end, nearing it by every step, but now, under the Gospel, that course has (if I may so speak) altered its direction, as regards His second coming, and runs, not towards the end, but along it, and on the brink of it; and is at all times equally near that great event, which, did it run towards it, it would at once run into. Christ, then, is ever at our doors.[12]

Thus the Methodist Report is firmly grounded in reputable contemporary theology when it says:

The sacrament is an act of remembrance by which through the renewal of the corporate memory of the Church by the Holy Spirit, the great "salvation" events culminating in the Cross are re-enacted. This act of corporate recollection embraces not only the past but the future and what lies beyond history in the consummation of the Kingdom of God.[13]

Moreover, so far from being an uncritical disciple of Dom Gregory Dix, I remember some fifteen years ago in Oxford withstanding that lovable saint to this face and saying that what

[11] *The Apostolic Preaching and Its Developments* (New York: Harper & Row, 1936), p. 256.
[12] *Parochial and Plain Sermons*, VI (London: Longmans, Green & Company, 1896), 240-41.
[13] P. 32.

he meant Christianly by the Mass was what I meant by "justification by faith alone."

And I took him to task for his garbled account of the Reformation and its liturgies: the way in which, for example, when he describes events in Wittenberg in 1522 he compresses into three weeks events which took place in the whole of Germany over five years and some which never took place at all. I agreed with his perception that the Cranmer eucharist is the liturgical expression of justification "sola fide," but said that, of course, he completely misunderstands the meaning of "sola fide." For in fact Dix at this point capsizes his own argument, and he charges the reformers with intending by "anamnesis" that bare mental recollection of the absent past which he denied was what it meant in the early church.

Now I do not deny that there have been times and places in Protestant history when such a view has appeared. I remember seeing a conservative evangelical Anglican college in Australia where over the communion table were the words, "He is not here!" The sixteenth-century view of heaven made it possible for the memorial of the Lord to be like the memory of some veteran of the Old Guard, of an exiled Napoleon perched in a distant St. Helena. I grant there are sentences of Cranmer, which taken out of their context, isolated from his view of our incorporation into Christ through baptism, and his view of saving faith, could be made to sound like this.

B. S. Childs suggests that it may have been some dire historic crisis of near apostasy which turned Israel to its living remembrance of its kerygmatic past. Is not this what happened to the sixteenth-century reformers? [14]

[14] Late mediaeval eucharistic theology in Gabriel Biel (Heiko Oberman, *The Harvest of Medieval Theology* [Cambridge: Harvard University Press, 1963]), in Johannes Eck (E. Iserloh, *Die Eucharistie in der Darstellung des Johannes Ecks* [Munster: Aschendorff, 1950], and in Cajetan (F.

The reformers returned to justification by "only faith" because it is a theology of the Cross and of the Word. All the reformers, of right and left, did two things. They rejected the idea of the sacrifice of the Mass, as doing Calvary again, and the idea of faith as a "fides historica." The latter is what Tyndale called a "story-book faith" which is like believing the histories of Julius Caesar. For the reformers "remembrance" in faith can never be mere intellectual recollection alone.

Here is Andrew Karlstadt, the high point of subjectivism, but even he says:

> The Lord's Supper is the memorial (Gedächtnis) and preaching (Verkündigung) of the death of Christ, yet this memorial cannot be without faith and the knowledge of Christ, any more than I could remember my father unless I have known him . . . and so this remembering is bound up with our knowing and believing—the more fervent and clear is our knowledge of Christ, the more devout and clear is our memorial—if it is only hearsay faith it all becomes trivial.[15]

He even adds, "Remembering can justify."

When Luther trounces this a year later, it is also to stress the present objectivity of the Presence. "If I were to remember Christ with such warmth and remembrance that I sweat blood, it would all amount to nothing, for it would all be in the realm of works and commandments, and there would be no Gift, no Word of God who reaches out and gives me Christ's Body and Blood." [16]

---

Clark, *Eucharistic Sacrifice and the Reformation* [Westminster, Md.: Newman Press, 1960]; E. L. Mascall, *Corpus Christi* [London: Longmans, Green & Company, 1953]) may have been more respectable than is often supposed, but it is notable how much of it is now discarded by such modern Catholics as De Taille, Masure, Vonier, and Casels, and no reputable historian could today deny the flagrant abuse and malpractice which centered in the Mass.

[15] *Karlstadts Schriften*, Herztsch, ed. Part 2 (1957), p. 27.
[16] *Weimar Ausgabe*, XVIII, 195, 23.

Zwingli strengthens the word "Gedächtnis" to avoid this misunderstanding,

The Mass is not a sacrifice, but it is a remembering (Wiedergedächtnis) of the sacrifice offered once for all, so powerful and present to us at all times is Christ.

If the Holy Sacrament is not a sacrifice, yet it is a remembrance (Wiedergedächtnis) and a renewal (Erneuerung) of what happened once for all and is eternally mighty and precious.[17]

Werner Krusche gives a whole series of passages where Calvin speaks of the blood of Christ as made present by the work of the Holy Spirit. "Jesus Christ was offered once for all . . . but the power of that oblation lasts for ever. It is permanent. And so the blood of Jesus Christ is freshly given for us. . . . It does not cease to flow, it does not dry up, but it washes our souls daily through the power of the Holy Spirit."[18]

Behind Calvin here are the fathers, as alongside Zwingli stood Oecolampadius with his love of the Greek fathers, and Melanchthon beside Luther with his appeal to the Testimonia Patrum.[19]

Professor Orcibal of the Sorbonne has drawn attention to the ecumenical movement which went on in the late seventeenth century in which Protestants and Catholics, Jansenists, and non-Jurors shared a common circle of devotional ideas. Part of this was the patristic learning of the generation of Samuel Wesley, and it is this which gives significance to the three eucharistic writings which John Wesley took with him to

[17] "Exposition and Ground of the 67 Articles," in *Auswahl seiner Schriften*, Künzli, ed. (1962), p. 100.
[18] *Das Wirken des heiligen Geistes nach Calvin* (1957), p. 158.
[19] P. Fraenkel, *Testimonia Patrum* (Geneva: 1961). See also P. Polman, *L'Elément Historique dans la Controverse Religieuse du XVI Siecle* (Gembloux: J. Ducúlot, 1932).

Georgia: his father's *Pious Communicant,* John Johnson's *Unbloody Sacrifice,* and Daniel Brevint's *Christian Sacrament and Sacrifice.*

Brevint, himself a high churchman and friend of the nonjurors but trained and exercised in the French Reformed ministry consciously set out to write of the sacrament in a way which cut across traditional boundaries. "Here," he says, "I take no more notice of either Papists or sectaries, no, nor Protestants." Some of Charles Wesley's sacramental hymns are simply versification of Brevint. Others have no relation to Brevint at all. From my own recent collation of John's abridgment with the original tract I can say that Charles Wesley's hymns are based on the original Brevint and not John Wesley's abridgment and alterations.

Brevint's view of "memorial" is exactly what we have been expounding. It is "not the bare Remembrance of his passion; but over and above, to invite us to his Sacrifice, not as done and gone many Years since, but, as to Grace and Mercy still lasting, still new, still the same as when it was first offered for us." [20] Here are just a few samples of this view in the hymns:

> But Jesu's death is ever new,
> He whom in ages past they slew
>   Doth still as slain appear.

> The blood doth now as freely flow,
> As when his side received the blow
>   That show'd him newly dead

> Thy offering still continues new,
> Thy vesture keeps its bloody hue.

We saw that Calvin at this point brings in the Holy Spirit. And here Charles Wesley brings in an important theme which

[20] *The Christian Sacrament and Sacrifice,* Section II, No. 7.

183

has no counterpart in Brevint. This "anamnesis" is no mere human recollection, because, in fact, it takes place only by the Holy Spirit. And he takes two traditional English words, the thought of a Recorder, and a Remembrancer, and he brings them together:

> Come, Thou everlasting Spirit,
>   Bring to every thankful mind
> All the Saviour's dying merit,
>   All His sufferings for mankind:
>
> True Recorder of His passion
>   Now the living faith impart,
> Now reveal His great salvation,
>   Preach His gospel to our heart.
>
> Come, Thou Witness of His dying;
>   Come, Remembrancer divine,
> Let us feel Thy power, applying
>   Christ to every soul, and mine.

Some of us got our Catholicity, not from high Anglicans but from a Congregationalist, Bernard Manning. Manning once described

the pitiful ruin of Bardney Abbey, left as Henry VIII and his followers left it. . . . You may see . . . unharmed . . . the altar of the five wounds of Christ, . . . one in each corner and one in the centre. Who thought of this or the five wounds in eighteenth-century England? . . . Within a stone's-throw of the altar of the five wounds, the Methodists were singing: . . .

> Turn to Jesus crucified,
>   Fly to those dear wounds of His.
>
> . . . . . . . . . . .
> Five bleeding wounds He bears,

> Received on Calvary;
> They pour effectual prayers,
> They freshly plead for me.[21]

But at this point the Methodists join word and sacrament. Turn to two of John Wesley's most famous sermons, on justification by faith (V) and the righteousness of faith (VI) and observe how at the climax he sets forth the Cross as present: "Thus look to Jesus. There is the Lamb of God, who taketh away thy sins." [22] "Look unto Jesus. Behold, how He loveth thee! . . . O Lamb of God, . . . was ever love like thine?" [23] It is all there in the classic definition of Methodist preaching: "To invite, to convince, to offer Christ . . . to preach him in all his offices . . . [to] set forth Christ as evidently crucified before their eyes, . . . justifying us by his blood, and sanctifying us by his spirit." [24]

Word and sacrament: sacramental and evangelical. Here is how one of these very hymns played its part in the conversion of one of the preachers, Thomas Tennant.

However, at last, as a poor, weary, heavy-laden sinner, who had nothing to plead, but "God be merciful to me for Christ's sake," I ventured to eat of that bread, and drink of that cup. Just before I came up to the table, these words were deeply impressed upon my mind,—

> "Covered with Thy blood we are:
> Find a part that does not arm,
> And strike the sinner there."

[21] The Hymns of Wesley and Watts (London: The Epworth Press, 1942), pp. 132-33.

[22] Wesley's Standard Sermons, Edward H. Sugden, ed., I (Nashville: Methodist Publishing House, 1935), 130.

[23] Ibid., p. 144.

[24] From Minutes of Several Conversations between John Wesley and the Preachers in connexion with him, 1797. Answer to question 19.

. . . I rose from the table with a glad heart, greatly rejoicing in God my Saviour.[25]

Sacrifice is one of the great images of the work of Christ. We must be careful not to allegorize the parable, which is what we do when we make an elaborate analysis of what is entailed in sacrifice and then apply it to the Cross and to the eucharist. This is what the fathers of the Council of Trent seem to have done, and is what was done by F. C. N. Hicks in a luminous book, *The Fullness of Sacrifice*.[26] Mr. Beckwith treats the studies of Vincent Taylor[27] with horror, as the one who may have prepared Methodists for their capitulation to Gregory Dix. But my generation is not ashamed to confess to have learned from the integrity and careful scholarship of a great Methodist, as I have also valued C. H. Dodd's studies in "ilaskesthai" and "orge" though they were perhaps a little too good to be true.[28] And then I am a devotee of Alexander Nairne's *Epistle of Priesthood*,[29] so that if I could only take one epistle on a desert island it would be the Epistle to the Hebrews.

Though there is not in it all the range of New Testament truth about the death of Christ, and it does not mention "dikaioun" or dwell on the overruling love and grace of God, yet to its profound awareness of the inseparability of the finality of person and work in Christ we most fruitfully turn.

The Report asserts the finished work of Christ and denies "that we can add to it by anything we do, or that it needs to be done again. . . . The background . . . is the sacrifice of Christ, and

[25] *The Lives of the Early Methodist Preachers*, Thomas Jackson, ed., VI (London: Wesleyan Conference Office, 1873), 237.

[26] (London: The Macmillan Company, 1930).

[27] *Jesus and His Sacrifice* (London: The Macmillan Company, 1937).

[28] *The Bible and the Greeks* (London: Hodder & Stoughton, 1934).

[29] (Edinburgh: T. & T. Clark, 1913).

Christ alone, on the Cross. It is that we represent and re-present and renew by our remembrance and communion." [30]

There can be no going back on Cranmer's mighty line: "He made there by his one oblation of himself once offered, a full, perfect and sufficient sacrifice, satisfaction and oblation for the sins of the whole world." But can we not also sing with Charles Wesley in his greatest eucharistic hymn:

> With solemn faith we offer up,
>   And spread before Thy glorious eyes,
> That only ground of all our hope,
>   That precious, bleeding sacrifice,
> Which brings Thy grace on sinners down,
>   And perfects all our souls in one.

There is a problem here, which is posed by another great hymn:

> Entered the holy place above,
>   Covered with meritorious scars,
> The tokens of his Dying love
>   Our great High-priest in glory bears;
> He pleads His passion on the tree,
> He shows Himself to God for me.

Is this thought of Christ eternally pleading for us really scriptural? Well, if we are to stop singing Charles Wesley, we must drop Isaac Watts, too, for the same thought comes in one of his greatest verses.

> Jesus, my great High-priest,
>   Offered his blood and died;
> My guilty conscience seeks

[30] P. 32.

187

No sacrifice beside;
His powerful blood did once atone,
And now it pleads before the throne.

Against this there is the authority of a famous passage by
Westcott in his *Commentary on Hebrews* 8:3. "The modern
conception of Christ pleading in heaven his passion, offering his
blood on behalf of men has no foundation in the Epistle. His
glorified humanity is the eternal pledge of the absolute efficacy of his accomplished work. He pleads, as older writers
truly expressed the thought, by his presence upon the Father's
throne." [31]

It would be interesting to know what Westcott meant by
"modern," for passages could be quoted from Luther and from
Calvin to support Wesley and Watts. But Westcott's valid
point is supported also by a well-known passage from H. B.
Swete:

Jesus is not to be thought of as an "orante" standing ever before
the Father with outstretched arms like the figures in the mosaics of
the catacombs and with strong tears and crying pleading our cause
in the presence of a reluctant God, but as a throned Priest-King
asking what he will from a Father who always hears and grants his
requests: Our Lord's life in heaven is his prayer.[32]

But how then shall we interpret "he ever liveth to make intercession for us? What is "Our Lord's life in heaven"? How are
we to think of the even greater mystery—"What goes on in
God?" What is a true image of the Blessed Trinity which can
reckon with the intercession of the Son, and also of the Holy
Ghost?

I am sure we must not ask the writer to the Hebrews ques-

[31] (Grand Rapids: Wm. B. Eerdmans, 1950), p. 235.
[32] *The Catholicity of Protestantism*, Flew & Davies, eds. (1950), p. 113.

tions he did not raise and would not have understood. What he says in Hebrews 8:3 is splendidly coherent with his argument in the previous chapter, with the contrast of the availing, once-for-all offering of our High Priest with the incessant and ineffectual offerings of a Levitical priesthood. Jesus has taken his throne once for all and for ever.

Nevertheless the image is one of a continuing priesthood as well as kingship. My colleague, F. F. Bruce, who follows Swete here, thinks we find the clue to our Lord's heavenly intercession in the Gospels, in the action of Jesus when he prayed for Peter, "If it be asked what form his heavenly intercession takes what better answer can be given than that he still does for his people at the right hand of God what he did for Peter on earth." [33]

But why only what he did for Peter? Why not what he did for us all? Why only his word, and not his greatest deed? I find a deeper truth in James Moffatt's comment on the same verse—"His intercession . . . has red blood in it." [34] And I find some help in the great saying of Léon Bloy: "Suffering, that passes: to have suffered, that never passes."

And perhaps Hebrews does not take us all the way. Perhaps we who live in continuing time find a new problem which did not exist for his eschatological framework. We have to add to Hebrews, Romans 8:34, and more especially I John 2:1. And then there is Revelation. Whatever we do with Revelation 5:6 and 13:8, it still remains that the great emblem of our Savior is the Lamb, glorified as Lord and Leader, but still surely not only Eternal Priest, but Eternal Victim? It is always rather rash to accuse Charles Wesley and Isaac Watts of being un-

[33] *Commentary on Hebrews, New International Commentary* (Grand Rapids: Wm. B. Eerdmans, 1965), p. 155.
[34] *Commentary on Hebrews, International Critical Commentary* (Edinburgh: T. & T. Clark, 1924), p. 100.

scriptural. I think we may agree with Bernard Manning that in this verse there is profound and vigorous orthodoxy:

> Victim divine, Thy grace we claim,
>> While thus Thy precious death we show:
> Once offered up, a spotless Lamb,
>> In Thy great temple here below,
> Thou didst for all mankind atone,
> And standest now before the throne.
>
> Thou standest in the holy place,
>> As now for guilty sinners slain:
> The blood of sprinkling speaks, and prays,
>> All prevalent for helpless man;
> Thy blood is still our ransom found,
> And speaks salvation all around.

Finally, the Report on Conversations between the Church of England and the Methodist Church speaks of an offering of ourselves and adds that "the reality of the offering of ourselves . . . will be determined by the degree to which we become united to Christ in his death." [35]

Mr. Beckwith says this confuses Christ's work with ours. Indeed, he complains, "It is common today to find not only Anglo-Catholics but Presbyterians, Baptists, and Congregationalists asserting that our self-oblation is identical with Christ's." [36]

This is the place to dig one's toes in and to stand firmly by T. W. Manson when he said:

It will not do to create artificial distinctions between the self sacrifice of Christ and the self sacrifice of Christians. For obedience

[35] P. 32.
[36] *Priesthood and Sacraments*, p. 86.

is one and indivisible. . . . We conserve the uniqueness of the high-priesthood of Christ, not by shutting it away in splendid isolation, but by declaring and demonstrating its power to create and comprehend in itself a true priesthood of believers, whose priestly service is taken up into and made part of his supreme sacrifice.[37]

I do not find this far from Thomas Cranmer's prayer that without respect of persons God would accept the sacrifice of every man—priest and lay person, English, French, Scot, Greek, Latin, Jew, and Gentile—according to his faithful and obedient heart.

And I can go on with William Temple: "The eucharist is a sacrifice, but we do not offer it: Christ offers it, and we responding to his act take our parts or shares in His one sacrifice as members of His body: Christ in us presents us with Himself to the Father: we in Him yield ourselves to be so presented." [38]

I am sorry for the Church of England, that at its two extremes there are two theologies of the cross, an evangelical one of the word believed and preached, the other of the sacraments. I am humbly proud that in our Methodist tradition the two are one.

But this is, finally, a problem before us all. At no point is the Christian tradition further removed from the world of modern man than in its speech about atonement, justification, and the eucharist. The problem before the church, as it was in the second and in the fourth and fifth centuries, is how to translate truth without slipping into a fatal Gnosticism, a capitulation to the prevailing world view. Meanwhile it is essential to the mission of the church that it keep the polarity

[37] *Ministry and Priesthood: Christ's and Ours* (Richmond: John Knox Press, 1959), p. 63. See also C. F. D. Moule, *The Sacrifice of Christ* (Philadelphia: Fortress Press, 1964), pp. 45-57.
[38] *Christus Veritas* (London: Macmillan & Co., 1926), p. 243.

between the word and faith, between the "once-for-all" and the "now" of its gospel.

As the pilgrim church moves through history each moment is for it the "now" in which all salvation is concentrated, and all that has to be saved is centered. There are the new sins, the new crimes, not only of individuals but of cities and nations, and not only of nations, but of the people of God: from the sack of Rome to the Nuremberg war crimes, the Sicilian vespers to the massacre of Polish soldiers at Katin, the Crusades to Hiroshima, and added to all these, the vast tale of unrecorded wrongs, unknown to men but all marked down by God from the blood of Abel to the last cry of the poor man, the widow, and the fatherless. And this is how it will go on, tomorrow and tomorrow and tomorrow, till the last syllable of recorded time. And against each moment of it, what is there but the little phrase—the scandalon—*per Jesum Christum Dominum Nostrum*, which yet is the fulcrum of the universe, for it is not divine power, or even divine authority, but divine love which moves the sun and the other stars, infinite and boundless compassion. And we men of the church, this Ship of Fools, this Noah's Ark? Our only virtue is that we know where to go, we know where to turn, we know what we have to say. And whether we sing it, as it is indeed worthy to be sung, by Bach and Beethoven or the atheist Janicek—or say it with our own poor, lisping, stammering tongues, this is the heart of it all, this the availing prayer.

"O Lamb of God, who takest away the sins of the world, have mercy upon us."

# 9

## CHRIST AND CHRISTIANITY

The reader has the right to ask a concluding question. It is the same question many people have voiced with regard to the Institute at which these papers were read and discussed. That question is: Did you come to any conclusions? Is there any agreement as to what is the Christian claim regarding the finality of Jesus Christ?

One would hardly expect total consensus from a group of working theologians. Generally, they are persons characterized by probing, creative minds. Most of them are teachers accustomed to the responsibility of exposing the student to many sides of every problem. Therefore, a tight agreement on any doctrine of the church among such a group would not only be a surprise, it would deserve to be suspect.

The problem of stating the claims regarding Christ is not, however, to be explained by the variant characteristics of theological professors. The whole history of doctrine is evidence enough of the inherent difficulties involved in defining and stating the nature of the claims for Christ.

There is, however, one statement of consensus which can be made with confidence. *Christ is crucial for Christianity.* However differently the definitions are made and debated, parties involved do agree that Christianity must take its definition from the nature of Christ himself. For this religion Christ is final. Whatever he was or is, is what the religion about him becomes.

The diversity of opinion about Jesus Christ is not found only among theologians, but is just as diverse among lay Christians. It would be enlightening, perhaps shocking, for any local church pastor to conduct an institute among the lay members of his congregation on the finality of Jesus Christ. They have at some time or other in their lives answered affirmatively the question put to them in baptism or confirmation: "Do you confess Jesus Christ as your Lord and Savior?" Papers written on what this means to them would quite possibly reveal a wider spectrum than found even among professional theologians.

The modern churchman lives in the modern world. Impulses which figure into the formation of his attitudes and opinions come to him largely from a nonchurch context. Whether this is good or bad could be a subject for extensive debate, but need not be so here. That it is a fact will scarcely be questioned.

Whatever the mood of other generations may have been, our present one is not one naturally congenial to the traditional claims for Christ made by his church. The contemporary mind values highly the nondogmatic stance. It is suspicious of any and all dogmatisms. This results, understandably, from commitments to freedom of thought and expression, from a liberal spirit which makes large room for tolerance of persons who hold opposing views, and from the pluralism of modern society. It also is characteristic of a man who avoids individual involvement and commitment. If the pursuit of truth can be kept an open-ended process, with heavy emphasis on the virtue of objectivity, a person may avoid the agony of choice and the responsibilities of personal commitment.

Western man at the present time expresses himself in much the same manner non-Christian religions state some of their beliefs. The other religions have little attraction for him as a substitute for his own cultural type of Christianity, largely because they, too, carry with them a culture. The cultural accretions of Buddhism, Hinduism, Islam, and others are still so foreign to Western man that he is not really a candidate for conversion. He does, however, find it easier often to agree with them than with the claims of Christianity.

When Dr. Ratanasara characterizes Siddhartha Gautama he does it in words congenial to many Methodist laymen. "At no time did the founder of this system of thought expect his followers to regard him as a divine being. He never asked his disciples to believe anything he said without appealing to their reason. His attitude to knowledge was absolutely liberal. Freedom of thought, freedom of speech, respect for other peoples' views, and tolerance of other systems of thought, were his most outstanding features." Many church school teachers would prefer that attitude to Jesus' statement, "No one comes to the Father, but by me" (John 14:6).

Sikhism was born in the fifteenth century but its proponents sound completely modern when stating, as Mrs. Wylam does, "The Guru maintained that God can reveal himself to man through all religions. One of the fundamental precepts of the Sikh religion is tolerance and respect for all other faiths, even where there is disagreement on details of belief. . . . Whether man receives this relevation of God depends on his own efforts. . . . Mankind continues now, to be as diverse as he was in the past, and, although there is a certain merging of cultures and races in the modern world, it is not likely that all mankind *will* ever come under the spiritual sway of one special religion. Nor would this be a desirable state of affairs. . . . This being so, there is no justification for any one religious group to claim that theirs is the only true way to salvation and that it is only by following their particular master that all mankind can be saved."

Even pastors may find themselves wanting to believe that this is what Paul meant when he said, "In past generations he allowed all the nations to walk in their own ways; yet he did not leave himself without witness" (Acts 14:16).

Christianity seems to be faced with an anomalous situation. Large numbers of persons in the Christian church find themselves more in agreement with certain basic positions of the non-Christian religions than with the claims of their own faith. This seems to have resulted from the high degree of influence of the modern secular mind on the mind of the churchman. If this be a correct analysis, it means that Western secularism and Eastern religions are in closer agreement with each other than either is with traditional Christianity.

Dr. Will Herberg rightly insisted that his chapter on the Jew and the Christian claim for Christ not be grouped with Buddhism and Sikhism as a "counter-claim." He makes the claim that "Judaism and Christianity . . . represent one faith expressed in two religions—Judaism facing inward to the Jews, and Christianity facing outward to the gentiles. . . . The Jew sees Jesus as emerging from Israel and going forth; he sees him from the rear, as it were. The Christian, on the other hand, precisely because he is a Christian, will see Christ as coming toward him."

The theological task in our time gives a large place to the attempt to clarify the biblical claims regarding Christ. The primary question is to try to determine whether they reflect Jesus' self-understanding or the church's experience of him. Dr. Niles in examining the biblical testimony points out that the Christian Scriptures differ from the claims of all other faiths in that the coordinates within which the graph of the Christian faith is placed differ from the coordinates of other systems of belief. "The very act of faith is different." Christians believe in a different way. This must be understood before one moves

196

into the biblical claims. Miss Hooker makes her case for believing that in the "Son of Man" concept we are closest to Jesus' own self-understanding, though she readily admits that this view has recently come under the strongest kind of attack.

The Reverend David Jenkins has clearly in mind the new dimensions which in a space age affect man's thinking about Jesus Christ. "We need, and have the opportunity for, a new understanding of the cosmic significance of Jesus which will match our modern understanding of the cosmos. Unless this understanding of Jesus and the modern understanding of the cosmos are brought together, we shall be failing in preaching the gospel for our age, and we shall also be leaving humanity to be swamped in the apparent vastness and indifference of that cosmos as we are now coming to understand it." It is possible to do this, he says, by using the word and wisdom language of scripture and the process language of philosophy.

Though it is essential that the church constantly clarify its understanding of the scriptural claims, it must then take cognizance of the fact that these claims cannot be communicated to modern man as scriptural claims. For this man quite probably does not recognize the authority of Scripture as the church itself does.

If the biblical claim about Jesus is accepted as valid by the true Christian believer, and if he acknowledges an obligation to communicate this claim to those who do not accept it, how can such a claim be stated so as to be convincing to the contemporary mind? The answer to this question would appear to be significant to the task of evangelism, the task of missions, the task of apologetics, the task of social witness, the task of theological education, and, of course, to the whole task of the local congregation and the Christian man.

The problem of communication does not begin, however,

with the hearer, but with the proclaimer. An uncertainty in the initial witness will be amplified into confusion when it reaches the world outside the church. It is fundamentally, psychologically, sound that since the church defines itself as Christian, uncertainty about Christ will seriously distort, if not destroy, its message. The alternative is not rigid dogmatism. Intolerance is a sure sign of uncertainty; it does not convey the message to the unbeliever. There is a false holding of truth which results in failure to communicate. This falseness may be either the shallow tolerance which refuses to define Christ clearly or the strident dogmatism which loses the essential Christ in statements about him which lack his Spirit. The confidence of a believing church should arise out of knowing Christ in an essential definition of his nature which reveals his true Spirit.

The claim is here being made that the church must know in what sense Jesus Christ is final. Such a claim must involve the following elements:

1. To know Jesus Christ is to know God in a way not available in any other revelation.
2. What is available to be known in Jesus is all that man needs to know about God.
3. The whole event of Jesus Christ defines essential human nature. Any man who reaches the true goal of human existence will have done so by approximating the humanity of Jesus.
4. The above claims are not only made valid, but made available to all men by the unique aliveness of Jesus Christ in man's experience.
5. Man's history is finally judged by its approximation to the nature of God whose nature is revealed in Jesus Christ.

If these be accepted as essential elements of the definition of Christ's finality, their clarity need not be surrendered because of the acknowledged fact that endless debates flow out of them.

198

These definitions of Christ can be held at a primary level, and the definitions of the definitions must be held at a secondary level where the debates will always be needed. Is it valid, therefore, to suggest that there is a distinction between "definitions of Christ" and "definitions of the definitions"?

For example, element 1 and element 3 were the issues which produced Nicaea and Chalcedon. "Christian thinkers must necessarily obey the restless impulse to seek words and phrases which will express with all possible clarity what the church has always known to be true of Jesus Christ: the singularity of his person and the comprehensiveness of his saving life," says J. Robert Nelson. The Christian will have difficulty in any generation choosing precise words in trying to explicate the manner in which God could be three persons or the manner in which Jesus could be man and God. The difficulty at this level, however, must not cloud the Christian's primary definition that to know Jesus Christ is to know God and essential human nature.

Vigorous debate always attends the statement of element 4, that the claims are validated and made available by the aliveness of Jesus. This debate has never been more vigorous than in our present generation.

This debate at the level of the definition of this definition is seen clearly in the preceding chapters. The vigor of it cannot be discerned from these pages, but can only be known to those who were present when the personalities of David Jenkins and Carl Michalson met. The basis of the gospel, says Jenkins, "lies in the actual life and death of Jesus understood against the Jewish expectations of God emerging from the experience of their history—with the defining dimension of this understanding provided by the discovery of the disciples that the crucified servant of the kingdom of God was in fact powerfully alive. If the disciples' discovery that Jesus was alive as a continuing power and presence central to their relationship with God was not a real discovery of an objective fact but only an attitude of theirs, an interpretation which they put upon the facts, then we have no grounds for the further language about Jesus. In other words, the question of the objectivity and reality of the resurrection of Jesus is central to the whole logic of talking about Jesus. This is what the New Testament itself would lead us to expect. The believers who made the New Testament, or whose attitude is reflected in the New Testament, did not believe that they were simply telling a story about the world, man, and God with Jesus as a character in that story. The story they felt able to tell depended on the objective reality of the Resurrection. . . . It does violence to the whole logic of the New Testament use of mythology to give an account of the Christian faith which seeks to represent the Resurrection as simply part and, indeed, a symbolic and mythological part of the Christian story, i.e., of the attitude which Christians adopt to the world and of the story which they tell to represent that attitude. It may be the case that the Resurrection is and can only be myth and symbol. But in that case Christianity is untrue."

The contradiction which Dr. Michalson offered to this definition is based on his distinction between nature and history. " 'World' in the New Testament, then, is not a quasi-scientific construct, a cosmographic arena upon which history plays out its game. World is a dominantly historical reality, a matrix of relationships into which, when one is fitted, one derives the meaning of one's own existence. Yet, world is not a space which preexists one's participation in it." The fact of the Resurrection is in man's history, that is, in man's experience of it, and not in nature, in objectivity apart from the experience of it.

When the members of the Institute asked the two men to join in further discussion of their positions, Jenkins declared there was no way in which they could talk to each other. Language was being so misused by Michalson so as to make conversation impossible between them. They did, however, delight the members with an unforgettable afternoon. As radical as the clash appears between the two positions, is it not a clash at the level of a definition of a definition, rather than at the primary level of the definition of Christ? Both men were insisting, as the church must always insist, that claims about Christ are not only validated but made available to all men by the unique *aliveness* of Jesus Christ in man's experience.

There is a definite finality of Christ without which Christianity is not Christian. If the church surrenders that, it surrenders everything. It may carry on what it calls evangelism, mission, and witness, but none of them will communicate to the party of the second part, because the word has been lost by the party of the first part.

The receiver of the communication must, however, be as clearly understood as the proclamation itself. Before we speak we must listen. We must listen, as has been said, to the word spoken in Christ, but we must also listen to the word spoken by man out of Christ.

At first he will insist that he no longer hears the word spoken by the church because it is carried in language no longer in his vocabulary. Once he objected to theological words because they were big and unfamiliar, but more recently he has delighted in being taught polysyllabic words by the scientist. He complained that the expressions of the gospel were not at home in his daily world, but now he has himself become a specialist in his vocation so that he uses words at the office which are not understood at home by his own family.

The task of restatement is a legitimate demand on the modern church, but the objections of the secular man to the language of the gospel may be deeper than he himself knows or admits. Dr. Nelson says, "Probably few theologians would now maintain that the Chalcedonian decree *invariata* stands as an adequate statement of Christology. . . . But when there is a call to reject or revise the words and concepts of Chalcedon, we must ask whether the reality to which these refer is also being rejected or revised." Dr. John Cobb takes up the challenge to state the Christian claims about Christ in language modern man may find acceptable as a vehicle of truth. "From the very beginning Christians have affirmed that God was present to and in Jesus in a preeminent way. Furthermore, Christians have believed that this presence of God to and in Jesus involved the distinctive initiative of God and was not simply a function of the peculiar virtue of this man. The theological problems to which this conviction has given rise are notorious." The duality which represents the alternate formulas was resolved in an Alexandrine victory over the Antiochenes. Dr. Cobb regards this as unfortunate and explains the loss as a fault of language, at least in part. "They lost out in part because they had available to them no conceptuality for explaining how God could at his own initiative be genuinely present to and in a man without displacing some element in the personal humanity of that man." Then, he proposes his solution for the same problem which the church has in confronting the modern world. "The philosophy of Alfred North Whitehead offers us at this point new possibilities that have not yet been sufficiently explored." He, therefore, devotes his chapter to an attempt to indicate "how from a Whiteheadian perspective a Christian can affirm the special presence of God to and in a man without reducing the man's full personal responsible humanity on the one hand or minimizing the divine initiative on the other."

This is a legitimate enterprise. There may be other vehicles acceptable to the men of our time which can be enlisted in the effort to speak the word convincingly to them. Here again we must be aware of the distinction between the primary definition of Christ's finality and the secondary level of the definition of the definitions. To disagree about Whitehead is not the same as disagreeing about Jesus.

It was suggested earlier that the insistence of modern man that the language of the church is incomprehensible may not point only to a fault in the language of the church but in the language of secular man. This ought not be said often, lest it destroy our ability to listen, but it must be said. Otherwise, we may hear his words and think we have satisfied the need by confessing a guilt consciousness for our failure. What is called for is a deeper hearing until we know that man is saying something about man.

When we are able to engage in this deeper hearing, we should rejoice, for we are then at the point of the secular confirmation of the finality of Christ.

The ultimate question for an individual is not the objectivity of truth nor the objectivity of the world, including other individuals. These objectivities may be real, and they are accepted as real by most men. The ultimate truth for an individual is the truth which is real in his experience. Nothing is true for me unless it is true for me. If Jesus Christ is final for me, this finality must be known to me in my own experience.

The arena of truth is, therefore, in the nature of man. Whatever an individual believes will make him a true human being is what he accepts as true. Individuals are known by us all to define truth differently, to accept sometimes opposing propositions as true. Each one, however, accepts what he does accept, for the same reason another one accepts the opposite. Each person somehow is convinced that what he accepts as truth is that which will fulfill his nature.

The way in which an individual is saved from solipsism is to be bombarded by claims to acceptance from sources outside himself. If he chooses to believe tables are unreal, he will bump into tables which challenge his prior acceptance. The world is an other-complex which contends for entry into the world of the self-experience as truth. Because of this no man can ignore the claims other existences make on behalf of themselves. A claim made by the other-complex must be assessed by the self-experience.

One of the facts of life in this world is the existence in its history and in its present moment of the claim made with regard to Jesus of Nazareth. There it is. The factuality of the claim is as real as a table.

The mission of the Christian church is to see that no man is ever allowed to live and complete his search for truth without being confronted by this factuality. Any man's system of acceptable truth is incomplete and unsafe, and by that much untrue, if it has been accepted without being apprised of the existence of the claim for the finality of Jesus Christ.

The severest kind of judgment of God may be expected on his church at any point where it is giving itself to activities which do not intentionally go to the point of secularity in every man and confront his self-experience with the finality-definition of Jesus Christ which is a part of the other-complex.

The reason why the church may perform this mission in confidence is that the claim fits the need. Man needs to become true man. Jesus Christ is true man. The finality of Christ is that he is Final Man. He is what every man was meant to be, and what man in his true humanity wants to be. The "godness" in Jesus is unique in that he not only, like every man, is a product of the creative hand of God, but he is the creative hand of God "fleshed out" so that it can now reach into humanity and make it true.

When any individual experiences this he knows the end, that is, the meaning of all history, universal and cosmic. The

end has come into the present. The church has a language
which is adequate to carry the freight laid on it by the "finished
work of Christ." That language, as Dr. Rupp reminds us, is
the word and the sacraments. These are not given to the
church to be treasured in their outmoded accretions. They are
given because not only are they adequate, which the "slang"
of man isn't, but because they are renewable.

Rupert Davies of Bristol, who led the Bible studies in
Colossians, also summed up the conference. His closing words
amply sum up this volume:

> It is clear that we have reached no finality about the finality
> of Christ; we are still puzzled by the problems with which we came
> to Oxford. But there is no disposition among us to detract from
> the majesty of Christ; he stands before us as redeemer and saviour,
> of us and of all mankind, as Lord and judge; as the meaning of
> history, and the agent of God in creation, as the perfection of
> human life and the central figure of the coming consummation. We
> do not clearly know how to express our convictions. We are dis-
> contented with the categories of Chalcedon, but not much less
> discontented with other, more recently formulated, terms. Yet our
> abiding concern is to set Christ forth as Lord as truly and effec-
> tively as the Church has ever done throughout its history; and we
> are therefore the more committed, because we have been here
> together and here have worked together to find the way in which
> this can be done, the *thought-forms* in which we can make it clear
> to ourselves and to others, the *language* which we can use, and the
> *worship* which we can offer.

# The Contributors

*John B. Cobb, Jr.*—Ingraham Professor of Theology, School of Theology at Claremont, California

*Will Herberg*—Graduate Professor of Philosophy and Culture, Drew University, Madison, New Jersey

*Morna Hooker*—Lecturer in New Testament Studies, King's College, University of London, England

*David E. Jenkins*—Fellow and Chaplain of the Queen's College, Oxford, England; University Lecturer in Theology

*Dow Kirkpatrick*—Minister, First Methodist Church, Evanston, Illinois; Co-ordinator of the Oxford Conference of Methodist Theologians, Oxford, England, 1965

*Carl Michalson*—Late Andrew V. Stout Professor of Systematic Theology, Drew University, Madison, New Jersey

*J. Robert Nelson*—Professor of Systematic Theology, the School of Theology, Boston University, Boston, Massachusetts

*D. T. Niles*—Chairman, North District, Methodist Church, Ceylon; General Secretary, East Asia Christian Conference

*Havanpola Ratanasara*—Lecturer, Vidyalankara University of Ceylon

*Gordon Rupp*—Professor of Ecclesiastical History, University of Manchester, England

*Mrs. Pamela M. Wylam*—Editor of the quarterly *Sikh Courier*; Lecturer in Comparative Religion

207

# The Contributors

John H. Crook —*Anthropologist, Reader in Ethology, School of Biology, University of Bristol, England.*

W. H. Thorpe —*Emeritus Professor of Psychology and Ethology, University of Cambridge, England.*

Gordon Dunstan —*Professor of New Testament Studies, King's College, University of London, England.*

David A. Jackson —*Fellow and Chaplain of the Queen's College, Oxford, England (formerly Chaplain, Exeter University, England).*

C. A. Keele —*Emeritus Professor, University of London (formerly Chairman of the United Kingdom Section of the Society for the Protection of Animals, England).*

Lord Platt —*Physician (formerly President of the Royal College of Physicians and Chairman of the Nuffield Foundation, England).*

J. Richard Skues —*Reader in Comparative Religion, King's College, University of London, England.*

W. D. M. Paton —*Pharmacologist, Fellow of the Royal Society, Professor of Pharmacology, University of Oxford, England.*

Thomas A. Sebeok —*Professor of Linguistics and of Anthropology, Indiana University, U.S.A.*

Stephen R. L. Clark —*Lecturer in Moral Philosophy, University of Glasgow, Scotland.*

Frederick A. Winter —*Research Fellow, Department of Experimental Psychology, University of Cambridge, England.*